国际财务报告准则

国际财务报告准则第11号
——合营安排

（汉英对照）

中国会计准则委员会　组织翻译

中国财政经济出版社

图书在版编目（CIP）数据

国际会计准则. 第 11 号，合营安排：汉、英/中国会计准则委员会组织翻译. 北京：中国财政经济出版社，2012.12
（国际财务报告准则）
ISBN 978-7-5095-4144-9

Ⅰ. ①国⋯ Ⅱ. ①中⋯ Ⅲ. ①国际会计准则－汉、英 Ⅳ. ①F233.1

中国版本图书馆 CIP 数据核字（2012）第 287454 号

责任编辑：李　静　　　　　　　版式设计：康普宝蓝
封面设计：九州迅驰

中国财政经济出版社 出版

URL：http://ckfz.cfeph.cn
E-mail：ckfz@cfeph.cn

（版权所有　翻印必究）

社址：北京市海淀区阜成路甲 28 号　邮政编码：100142
发行处电话：88190406　财经书店电话：64033436
河北零五印刷厂印刷　各地新华书店经销
787×1092 毫米　16 开　8.25 印张　170 000 字
2013 年 1 月第 1 版　2013 年 1 月河北第 1 次印刷
定价：30.00 元
ISBN 978-7-5095-4144-9/F·3364
（图书出现印装问题，本社负责调换）
图字：01-2013-0573
本社质量投诉电话：010-88190744

International Financial Reporting Standards (IFRSs) together with their accompanying documents are issued by the International Accounting Standards Board (IASB):

30 Cannon Street, London, EC4M 6XH, United Kingdom.

Tel: +44 (0) 20 7246 6410   Fax: +44 (0) 20 7246 6411

Email: info@ifrs.org   Web: www.ifrs.org

ISBN 978-7-5095-4144-9

Copyright © 2012 IFRS Foundation

The IASB, the IFRS Foundation, the authors and the publishers do not accept responsibility for loss caused to any person who acts or refrains from acting in reliance on the material in this publication, whether such loss is caused by negligence or otherwise.

IFRSs (which include International Accounting Standards and Interpretations) are copyright of the International Financial Reporting Standards (IFRS) Foundation. The authoritative text of IFRSs is that issued by the IASB in the English language. Copies may be obtained from the IFRS Foundation Publications Department. Please address publication and copyright matters to:

IFRS Foundation Publications Department

30 Cannon Street, London, EC4M 6XH, United Kingdom.

Tel: +44 (0) 20 7332 2730   Fax: +44 (0) 20 7332 2749

Email: publications@ifrs.org   Web: www.ifrs.org

All rights reserved. No part of this publication may be translated, reprinted or reproduced or utilised in any form either in whole or in part or by any electronic, mechanical or other means, now known or hereafter invented, including photocopying and recording, or in any information storage and retrieval system, without prior permission in writing from the IFRS Foundation.

A review committee appointed by the IFRS Foundation has approved the Simplified Chinese translation of the International Financial Reporting Standards and related material contained in this publication. The Simplified Chinese translation is published by the Chinese Finance and Economics Publishing House in China with the permission of the IFRS Foundation. The Simplified Chinese translation is the copyright of the IFRS Foundation.

The IFRS Foundation logo, the IASB logo, the IFRS for SMEs logo, the "Hexagon Device", "IFRS Foundation", "eIFRS", "IAS", "IASB", "IASC Foundation", "IASCF", "IFRS for SMEs", "IASs", "IFRS", "IFRSs", "International Accounting Standards" and "International Financial Reporting Standards" are Trade Marks of the IFRS Foundation.

国际财务报告准则（IFRSs）及其配套文件由国际会计准则理事会（IASB）发布。
30 Cannon Street, London, EC4M 6XH, United Kingdom.
Tel：+44（0）20 7246 6410   Fax：+44（0）20 7246 6411
Email：info@ifrs.org
Web：www.ifrs.org

ISBN 978-7-5095-4144-9
Copyright © 2012 IFRS Foundation

对于任何因本出版物中的材料而采取或不采取行动所导致的损失（无论该损失是由疏忽还是其他原因引起的），国际会计准则理事会、国际财务报告准则基金会、作者及出版者将不承担任何责任。

国际财务报告准则（包括国际会计准则及其实施指南）的版权归国际财务报告准则基金会所有。经批准的国际财务报告准则由国际会计准则委员会以英文形式发布，您可以从国际财务报告准则委员的出版部门获取。有关出版物和版权事宜请按如下地址联系：

IFRS Foundation Publications Department
30 Cannon Street, London, EC4M 6XH, United Kingdom.
Tel：+44（0）20 7332 2730   Fax：+44（0）20 7332 2749
Email：publications@ifrs.org   Web：www.ifrs.org

版权所有。未经国际财务报告准则基金会事先书面允许，任何人不得以任何方式（目前已知的和今后发明的电子、机械或其他方式，包括影印和录音），或者以任何信息存储和检索系统翻译、翻印、复制或使用本书中的任何内容。

由国际财务报告准则基金会认可的审核委员会对本出版物中的国际财务报告准则及其他相关文件的简体中文译本进行了审核。国际财务报告准则基金会授权中国财政经济出版社出版此中文译本。此中文译本的版权归国际财务报告准则基金会所有。

国际财务报告准则基金会标识，国际会计准则委员会标识，中小主体国际财务报告准则标识："Hexagon Device"，"IFRS Foundation"，"eIFRS"，"IAS"，"IASB"，"IASC Foundation"，"IASCF"，"IFRS for SMEs"，"IASs"，"IFRS"，"IFRSs"，"International Accounting Standards"和"International Financial Reporting Standards"均为国际财务报告准则基金会的商标。

国际财务报告准则中文翻译审核专家组

组　　长：王　军　财政部党组副书记、副部长，中国会计准则委员会主席，博士生导师
副组长：余蔚平　财政部部长助理
组　　员：冯淑萍　全国人大常委会预算工作委员会副主任，中国会计准则委员会委员，博士生导师
　　　　　沈小南　全国社会保障基金理事会副理事长，中国会计准则委员会咨询专家
　　　　　杨　敏　财政部会计司司长，中国会计准则委员会秘书长
　　　　　汤云为　上海财经大学教授，上海市会计学会会长，博士生导师
　　　　　刘光忠　财政部会计司副司长，中国会计学会秘书长
　　　　　袁文辉　德勤华永会计师事务所技术部合伙人，中国会计准则委员会咨询专家
　　　　　支晓强　中国人民大学商学院副院长，副教授
　　　　　毛新述　北京工商大学商学院副院长，副教授
　　　　　陆建桥　财政部会计司准则二处处长，中国会计准则委员会咨询专家

出版说明

2011年，国际会计准则理事会先后发布了《国际财务报告准则第10号——合并财务报表》、《国际财务报告准则第11号——合营安排》、《国际财务报告准则第12号——在其他主体中权益的披露》和《国际财务报告准则第13号——公允价值计量》四项新准则，并对《国际会计准则第1号——财务报表列报》、《国际会计准则第19号——雇员福利》、《国际会计准则第27号——合并财务报表和单独财务报表》和《国际会计准则第28号——在联营企业和合营企业中的投资》四项准则进行了修订。除修订后的《国际会计准则第1号》于2012年7月1日生效外，上述其他新发布或修订的国际财务报告准则都将于2013年1月1日起生效。

我国2006年发布的企业会计准则体系实现了与国际财务报告准则的趋同。2010年，财政部又发布了《中国企业会计准则与国际财务报告准则持续趋同路线图》。为借鉴国际财务报告准则完善我国企业会计准则体系，实现中国准则与国际财务报告准则的持续趋同，中国会计准则委员会组织人员对国际会计准则理事会新发布或修订的上述八项准则进行了翻译。经国际财务报告准则基金会认可的中文翻译审核专家组审核，上述国际财务报告准则中文版是国际财务报告准则基金会认可的国际财务报告准则官方译本，为国际财务报告准则基金会的正式出版物。

在翻译审校过程中，财政部会计司陆建桥、高大平、朱琳、陈瑜、夏文贤、徐华新、林屾等同志对本书的译稿进行了校译。财政部会计司副司长、中国会计学会秘书长刘光忠和财政部会计司司长、中国会计准则委员会秘书长杨敏对全部译稿进行了审阅。本书最后由财政部部长助理余蔚平和财政部党组副书记、副部长、中国会计准则委员会主席王军审定。值此相关国际财务报告准则中文版出版之际，特别感谢国际财务报告准则中文翻译审核专家组以及中国财政经济出版社的有关同志为本书的翻译出版工作所付出的辛勤劳动！

中国会计准则委员会
2013 年 1 月

总目录

国际财务报告准则第 11 号——合营安排 ………………………… 1

《国际财务报告准则第 11 号——合营安排》结论基础 …………… 27

《国际财务报告准则第 11 号——合营安排》示例 ………………… 45

INTERNATIONAL FINANCIAL REPORTING STANDARD 11
JOINT ARRANGEMENTS ………………………………………… 54

BASIS FOR CONCLUSIONS ON IFRS 11 JOINT ARRANGEMENTS ………… 85

IFRS 11 JOINT ARRANGEMENTS ILLUSTRATIVE EXAMPLES ………… 109

《国际财务报告准则第 11 号 ——合营安排》

国际财务报告准则第11号——合营安排

目　录

	段落
引言	1–11

国际财务报告准则第11号——合营安排

	段落
目标	1–2
范围	3
合营安排	4–19
共同控制	7–13
合营安排类型	14–19
合营安排参与方的财务报表	20–25
共同经营	20–23
合营企业	24–25
单独财务报表	26–27

附录
　　附录一　术语定义
　　附录二　应用指南
　　附录三　生效日期、过渡性规定和其他国际财务报告准则的撤销

理事会批准 2011 年 5 月发布的《国际财务报告准则第 11 号》

《国际财务报告准则第 11 号——合营安排》由第 1 段至 27 段和附录一至附录四组成。所有段落均具有同等效力。以**粗体**标示的段落规定了主要原则。附录一给出了本准则中第一次出现的术语。其他术语的定义在国际财务报告准则的术语表中给出。《国际财务报告准则第 11 号》应结合其目标和结论基础、《国际财务报告准则前言》和《编报财务报表的框架》的内容一并阅读。在缺乏明确指南的情况下,《国际会计准则第 8 号——会计政策、会计估计变更和差错》规定了选择和应用会计政策的基础。

引言

概览

1. 《国际财务报告准则第 11 号——合营安排》为合营安排参与方提供了编制财务报告的原则。

2. 本国际财务报告准则取代了《国际会计准则第 31 号——合营企业中的权益》和《解释公告第 13 号——共同控制主体：合营者的非货币性投入》，并从 2013 年 1 月 1 日或以后日期开始的年度期间生效，允许提前采用。

发布本国际财务报告准则的原因

3. 本国际财务报告准则主要解决《国际会计准则第 31 号》两个方面的问题：第一，安排的结构是会计处理的唯一决定因素；第二，主体对共同控制主体中的权益可以选择不同的会计处理方法。

4. 《国际财务报告准则第 11 号》改进了《国际会计准则第 31 号》，建立了适用于所有合营安排的会计处理原则。

本国际财务报告准则的主要特征

5. 本国际财务报告准则要求参与合营安排的参与方根据对合营安排权利和义务的评估确定合营安排的类型。

总体要求

6. 本国际财务报告准则适用于参与合营安排的所有主体。合营安排是由两个或两个以上的参与方共同控制的一项安排。本国际财务报告准则将共同控制定义为，按合同约定分享对一项安排的控制权，并且仅在对相关活动（即对该安排的回报具有重大影响的活动）的决策要求分享控制权的参与方一致同意时才存在。

7. 本国际财务报告准则将合营安排分为两类——共同经营和合营企业。共同经营是指共同控制一项安排的参与方（即共同经营者）享有与安排相关资产的权利，并承担与安排相关负债的义务的合营安排。合营企业是共同控制一项安排的参与方（即合营者）对安排的净资产享有权利的合营安排。

8. 主体通过考虑其在参与的合营安排中的权利和义务来确定该合营安排的类型。主体通过考虑该安排的结构和法律形式、参与方同意的合营安排合同条款以及其他相关的事实和情况等评估其权利和义务。

9. 本国际财务报告准则要求共同经营者根据适用于特定资产、负债、收入和费用的相关国际财务报告准则确认和计量与其在该合营安排中权益相关的资产和负债（并确认相关的收入和费用）。

10. 本国际财务报告准则要求合营者确认一项投资，并根据《国际会计准则第 28 号——联营和合营企业中的投资》使用权益法对该投资进行会计处理，除非该主体根据《国际会计准则第 28 号》的规定豁免应用权益法。

11. 对合营安排具有共同控制的参与方的披露要求，由《国际财务报告准则第 12 号——在其他主体中权益的披露》予以规范。

国际财务报告准则第 11 号——合营安排

目标

1. 本国际财务报告准则的目标是,确定在共同控制的安排(即合营安排)中拥有权益的主体编制财务报告的原则。

实现目标

2. 为实现第 1 段提出的目标,本国际财务报告准则规定了"共同控制"的定义,要求参与合营安排的主体根据对其权利和义务的评估确定所参与合营安排的类型,并根据该合营安排类型对其权利和义务进行会计处理。

范围

3. 本国际财务报告准则适用于参与合营安排的所有主体。

合营安排

4. 合营安排是由两个或两个以上的参与方共同控制的一项安排。
5. 合营安排具有以下特征:
(1) 参与方受到合同安排的约束(参见应用指南第 2 段至 4 段)。
(2) 合同安排赋予两个或两个以上的参与方共同控制该合同安排(参见第 7 段至 13 段)。

6. 合营安排不是共同经营，就是合营企业。

共同控制

7. 共同控制，指按合同约定分享对一项安排的控制权，并且仅在对相关活动的决策要求分享控制权的参与方一致同意时才存在。

8. 作为合营安排参与方的主体应评估该合同安排是否使所有参与方或一组参与方集体控制该安排。如果所有参与方或一组参与方必须一致行动才能决定对该安排的回报具有重大影响的活动（即相关活动），则所有参与方或一组参与方集体控制该安排。

9. 一旦确定了所有参与方或一组参与方集体控制合营安排，当且仅当相关活动的决策要求集体控制该安排的这些参与方一致同意时，共同控制才存在。

10. 在合营安排中，任何一个参与方都不能单独控制该安排。对合营安排具有共同控制的任何一方均可以阻止其他参与方或一组参与方控制该安排。

11. 即使并非所有参与方对某一安排具有共同控制，该安排也可能是合营安排。本国际财务报告准则对共同控制合营安排的参与方（共同经营者或合营者）与参与但没有共同控制该安排的参与方进行了区分。

12. 主体对所有参与方或一组参与方是否共同控制安排进行评估时，需要运用判断。主体进行评估时应考虑所有事实和情况（参见应用指南第5段至11段）。

13. 如果事实和情况发生变化，主体应重新评估其是否对该安排具有共同控制。

合营安排的类型

14. 主体应确定其参与的合营安排的类型。将合营安排分类为共同经营或合营企业，取决于合营安排参与方的权利和义务。

15. 共同经营，是指共同控制一项安排的参与方享有与安排相关资产的权利，并承担与安排相关负债的义务的合营安排。这些参与方被称为共同经营者。

16. 合营企业，是指共同控制一项安排的参与方对安排的净资产享有权利的合营安排。这些参与方被称为合营者。

17. 主体在评估合营安排是共同经营还是合营企业时，需要运用判断。主体应根据其源于安排的权利和义务确定所参与的合营安排的类型。主体评估其权利和义务时，应当考虑安排的结构和法律形式、合同安排参与方认可的条款以及其他相关的事实和情况（参见应用指南第12段至33段）。

18. 主体有时会受到框架协议的约束，该协议规定了主体从事一项或多项活动需遵守的一般性合同条款。该框架协议可能规定，参与方为处理构成协议组成部分的特定活动应设立不同的合营安排。即使这些合营安排与同一框架协议相关联，如果参与方在从事框架协议涉及的不同活动中具有不同的权利和义务，那么，这些合营安排的类型也会有所差异。因此，当参与方从事同一框架协议中的不同活动时，共同经营和合营企业可能同时存在。

19. 如果事实和情况有所改变，主体应重新评估其参与合营安排的类型是否发生变化。

合营安排参与方的财务报表

共同经营

20. 共同经营者应确认与其在共同经营中权益相关的：
（1）资产，包括共同持有资产的份额；
（2）负债，包括共同承担负债的份额；
（3）销售其在共同经营产出中的份额获得的收入；
（4）在共同经营产出的销售收入的份额；
（5）费用，包括共同发生的费用的份额。

21. 共同经营者应根据适用于相关资产、负债、收入和费用的国际财务报告准则，对与其在共同经营中的权益相关的资产、负债、收入和费用进行会计处理。

22. 主体与其作为共同经营者的共同经营之间交易（例如，销售、投入或购买资产）的会计处理由应用指南第34段至37段规范。

23. 如果在安排中不具有共同控制的参与方享有共同经营相关资产的权利，并承担共同相关负债的义务，该参与方也应根据第20段至22段对其在该安排中的权益进行会计处理。如果在共同经营中不具有共同控制的参与方不享有共同经营相关资产的权利，也不承担共同经营相关负债的义务，该参与方应根据适用的国际财务报告准则对其在共同经营中的权益进行会计处理。

合营企业

24. 合营者应将其在合营企业中的权益确认为投资，并根据《国际会计准则第28号——在联营企业和合营企业中的投资》采用权益法对该项投资进行会计处理，除非合营者根据该准则的规定豁免应用权益法。

25. 参与合营企业但对其不具有共同控制的参与方应根据《国际财务报告准则第9号——金融工具》对其在安排中的权益进行会计处理，除非该参与方对合营企业具有重大影响，在这种情况下，主体应根据《国际会计准则第28号》（2011年修改）进行会计处理。

单独财务报表

26. 在单独财务报表中,共同经营者或合营者应:

(1) 根据第 20 段至 22 段对其在共同经营中的权益进行会计处理;

(2) 根据《国际会计准则第 27 号——单独财务报表》第 10 段对其在合营企业中的权益进行会计处理。

27. 在单独财务报表中,参与合营安排但对其不具有共同控制的参与方应:

(1) 根据第 23 段对其在共同经营中的权益进行会计处理;

(2) 根据《国际财务报告准则第 9 号》对其在合营企业中的权益进行会计处理,除非该主体对合营企业具有重大影响,在这种情况下,主体应适用《国际会计准则第 27 号》(2011 年修改) 第 10 段。

附录一　术语定义

本附录是本国际财务报告准则的组成部分。

合营安排	由两个或两个以上的参与方**共同控制**的一项安排。
共同控制	按合同约定分享对一项安排的控制权,并且仅在对相关活动的决策要求分享控制权的参与方一致同意时才存在。
共同经营	**共同控制**一项安排的参与方享有与安排相关资产的权利,并承担与安排相关负债的义务的合营安排。
共同经营者	对**共同经营**具有**共同控制**权的共同经营参与方。
合营企业	**共同控制**一项安排的参与方对安排的净资产享有权利的**合营安排**。
合营者	**共同控制**合营企业的**合营企业**参与方。
合营安排参与方	指参与**合营安排**的主体,无论该主体是否**共同控制**该安排。
单独主体	指单独可辨认的财务结构,包括单独的法律主体或由法规认可的主体,无论这些主体是否具有法人资格。

以下术语已在《国际会计准则第 27 号》(2011 年修改)、《国际会计准则第 28 号》(2011 年修改)或《国际财务报告准则第 10 号——合并财务报表》中予以定义,这些术语在本国际财务报告准则使用时的含义与上述国际财务报告准则的定义相同:
- 对被投资者的控制
- 权益法
- 权力
- 保护性权利
- 相关活动
- 单独财务报表
- 重大影响

附录二 应用指南

本附录是本国际财务报告准则的组成部分,规范了第1段至27段的应用,与本国际财务报告准则其他部分具有同等效力。

1. 本附录示例描述的是假设情况。尽管这些示例的有些方面可能以实际模式呈现,但在应用《国际财务报告准则第11号》时需要对特定实际模式的所有相关事实和情况进行评估。

合营安排

合同安排(第5段)

2. 合同安排可从几个方面证实。可执行的合同安排经常是(但并不总是)以书面的,通常采取合同形式或记录各方之间讨论的书面文件形式。法定机制本身或与参与方之间的合同相结合,也能产生可执行的安排。

3. 当合营安排通过单独主体构造而成时(参见应用指南第19段至33段),该合同安排或其中的某些方面,在一些情况下将包含在该单独主体所制定的条款、章程或规定中。

4. 合同安排设定了一些条款,以约束参与方参与的合同安排活动。合同安排一般涉及以下事项:

(1)合营安排的目的、活动和持续期间。

(2)合营安排的董事会或类似管理机构的成员的任命方式。

(3)决策程序:需要参与方决策的事务,参与方的表决权,对这些事务所要求的支持程度。合同安排中体现的决策程序形成了对该安排的共同控制(参见应用指南第5段至11段)。

(4)要求参与方提供的资本或其他投入。

(5)参与方分享或分担与合营安排相关的资产、负债、收入、费用或损益的方式。

共同控制(第7段至13段)

5. 主体在评估其是否共同控制一项安排时,首先应评估所有参与方或一组参与方是否控制该安排。《国际财务报告准则第10号》定义了控制的概念,也适用于确定所有参与方或一组参与方是否因涉入安排而有权获得可变回报,以及他们是否能够通过其对安排的权力影响这一回报。当从集体上考虑所有参与者或一组参与方被一致认为有能力主导对安排的回报具有重大影响的活动(即相关活动)时,这些参与方集体控制了该安排。

6. 主体在确定所有参与方或一组参与方集体控制该安排后,应评估其是否共同控制该安排。当且仅当相关活动的决策要求控制该安排的参与方一致同意时才存在共同控制。评估该安排是被所有参与方或一组参与方共同控制,还是被某一个参与方单独控制,需要进行判断。

7. 有时,由合同安排涉及的参与方一致同意的决策程序也可能导致共同控制。例如,假定两方建立一项安排,在该安排中双方各拥有50%的表决权。双方的合同安排规定,对相关活动作出决策至少需要51%的表决权。在这种情况下,意味着双方同意共同控制该安排,因为如果没有双方的同意,无法就相关活动作出决策。

8. 在其他情况下,合同安排规定了就相关活动作出决策所需要的最低表决权比例。如果存在多种参与方之间的联合能够满足最低表决权比例的要求需要与一联合方以上一起同意,该安排就不是合营安排,除非合同安排明确指明,需要其中哪些或多个参与方(或参与方的联合)一致同意后,才能就相关活动作出决策。

应用示例

例1

假定三方签订一项安排:A在该安排中拥有50%表决权,B拥有30%表决权,C拥有20%表决权。A、B、C之间的合同安排规定,对该安排相关活动的决定至少需要75%的表决权。尽管A能够否决所有决策,但是A没有控制该安排,因为A需要获得B的同意。合同安排条款要求至少需要75%表决权才能对相关活动作出决策,意味着A和B共同控制该安排,因为没有A或B的同意,就无法对相关活动作出决策。

例2

假定一项安排涉及三方:A在该安排中拥有50%的表决权,B和C各拥有25%的表决权。A、B、C之间的合同安排规定,对安排的相关活动作出决策至少需要75%的表决权。尽管A能够否决所有决策,但是A没有控制该安排,因为A需要获得B或C的同意。在本例中,A、B、C集体控制该安排。然而,存在多种参与方之间的联合能够达到75%表决权的要求(即A和B,或A和C)。在此情况下,三方签订的该合同安排要成为合营安排,需要在安排中指明,要求哪一种参与方之间的联合的一致同意才能对相关活动作出决策。

例 3

假定在一项安排中，A 和 B 各拥有 35% 的表决权，剩余 30% 的表决权由其他众多参与方拥有。对该安排的相关活动作出决策要求多数投票者的同意。当且仅当合同安排规定，相关活动的决策需要 A 和 B 一致同意时，A 和 B 才共同控制该安排。

9. 一致同意的要求意味着，共同控制该安排的任何参与方可以阻止其他任何参与方或一组参与方在不经其同意的情况下（就相关活动）单方面作出决策。如果一致同意的要求仅仅与向其中一个参与方提供保护性权利的决策有关，而与该安排的相关活动的决策无关，那么该参与方就不是该项安排的共同控制参与方。

10. 合同安排可能包括处理纠纷的条款，例如，仲裁。这些条款可能允许具有共同控制的各参与方没有达成一致意见情况下进行决策。这些条款的存在不会影响该安排的共同控制。因此，也不会妨碍该安排成为合营安排。

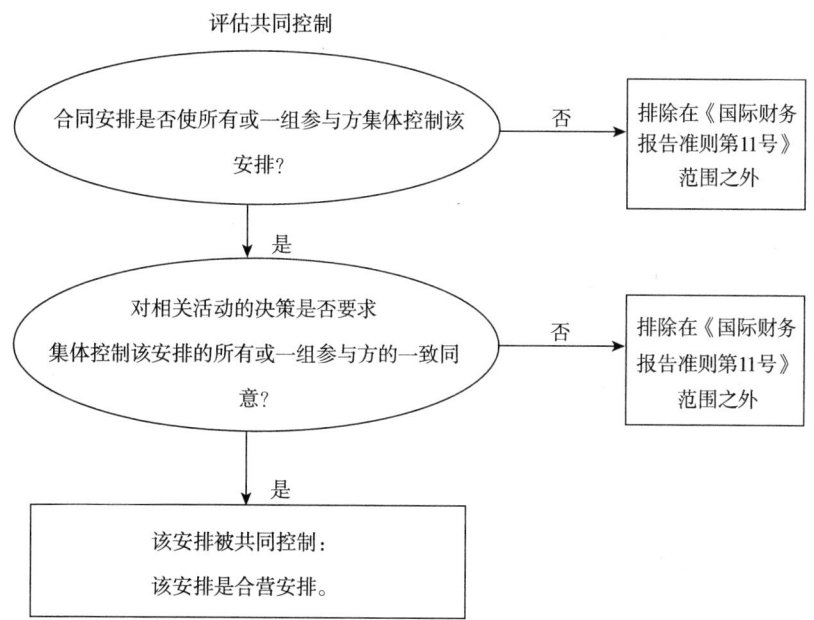

11. 当一项安排被排除在《国际财务报告准则第 11 号》范围之外，主体应根据相关国际财务报告准则，例如，《国际财务报告准则第 10 号》、《国际会计准则第 28 号》（2011 年修改）或《国际财务报告准则第 9 号》，对其在安排中的权益进行会计处理。

合营安排的类型（第 14 段至 19 段）

12. 合营安排是为不同目的而设立的（例如，参与方为了共同承担成本和风险，或者参与方为了获得新技术或新市场），可以采用不同的结构和法律形式。

13. 一些安排不要求采用单独主体的形式开展其活动。然而，其他安排涉及构造单独主体。

14. 本国际财务报告准则所要求的合营安排分类取决于各参与方在正常业务活动中从该安排享有的权利和承担的义务。本国际财务报告准则将合营安排分为共同经营和合营企业。当主体享有与安排相关资产的权利，并承担与安排相关负债的义务时，该安排就是共同经营。当主体对安排的净资产享有权利时，该安排就是合营企业。应用指南第 16 段至 33 段规范了主体为确定其是否在共同经营或合营企业中拥有权益所进行的评估。

合营安排的分类

15. 正如应用指南第 14 段指出，合营安排的分类需要各方评估其源于安排的权利和义务。在进行评估时，主体应考虑：
（1）合营安排的结构（参见应用指南第 16 段至 21 段）。
（2）当合营安排是通过单独主体构造时：
①该单独主体的法律形式（参见应用指南第 22 段至 24 段）；
②合同安排的条款（参见应用指南第 25 段至 28 段）；
③其他相关的事实和情况（参见应用指南第 29 段至 33 段）。

合营安排的结构

未通过单独主体构造的合营安排

16. 未通过单独主体构造的合营安排是共同经营。在这种情况下，根据合同安排，各参与方有权享有与该安排相关的资产、并承担对相关负债的义务，有权获得相应的收入、并对相应的费用承担责任。

17. 合同安排通常描述了该安排所从事活动的性质，以及各参与方打算共同承担这些活动的方式。例如，合营安排各参与方可能同意共同生产产品，每一参与方负责特定的任务，使用各自的资产，承担各自的负债。合同安排也可能规定了各参与方分享共同收入和分担共同费用的方式。在这种情况下，每一个共同经营者在其资产负债表上确认其用于完成特定任务的资产和负债，并根据合同安排确认相关的收入和费用份额。

18. 在其他情况下，例如，合营安排各参与方可能同意共同拥有和经营一项资产。在这种情况下，合同安排规定了各参与方对共同经营资产的权利，以及来自该项资产的收入或产出和相应的经营成本在各参与方之间分配的方式。每一共同经营者对其在共同资产中的份额、同意承担的负债份额进行会计处理，并按照合同安排确认其在产出、收入和费用中的份额。

通过单独主体构造的合营安排

19. 相关资产和负债由单独主体持有的合营安排，可能是合营企业，也可能是共同经营。

20. 参与方是共同经营者还是合营者，取决于该参与方对单独主体中持有的与安排相关的资产和负债的权利与义务。

21. 正如应用指南第 15 段指出，当各参与方通过单独主体构造合营安排时，各参与方需要评估该单独主体的法律形式、合同安排的条款以及其他相关的事实和情况是否赋予他们：

（1）享有与安排相关资产的权利，并承担与安排相关负债的义务（即该安排是共同经营）；或者

（2）享有安排的净资产的权利（即该安排是合营企业）。

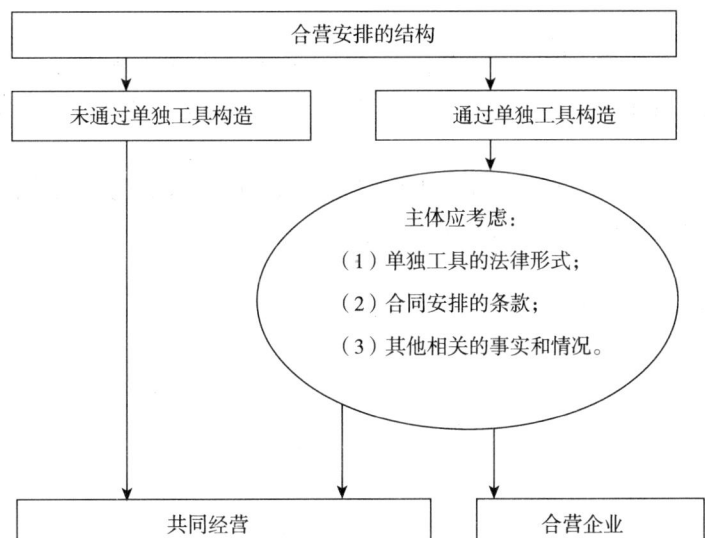

合营安排的分类：评估参与方源于安排的权利和义务

单独主体的法律形式

22. 当评估合营安排的类型时，单独主体的法律形式是相关的。法律形式有助于初步评估各参与方对单独主体中持有的资产享有权利，并对单独主体中持有的负债承担义务，例如，各参与方是否对单独主体持有的资产拥有权益，是否对单独主体持有的负债承担义务。

23. 例如，各参与方可能通过单独主体执行合营安排，单独主体法律形式导致考虑其自身权利（即在单独主体中持有的资产和负债是单独主体的资产和负债，而不是各参与方的资产和负债）。在这种情况下，单独主体的法律形式赋予各参与方权利和义务的评估表明，该项安排是合营企业。然而，各参与方在合同安排中同意的条款（参见应用指南第 25 段至 28 段），以及其他相关的事实和情况（参见应用指南第 29 段至 33 段）可以撤销基于单独主体的法律形式赋予各参与方权利和义务作出的评估。

24. 当且仅当各参与方为实施单独主体中合营安排，而单独主体法律形式上没有区分参与方和单独主体（即单独主体持有的资产和负债也是各参与方的资产和负债）时，基于单独主体法律形式赋予参与方权利和义务的评估足以说明该合营安排是共同经营。

评估合同安排的条款

25. 在许多情况下，各参与方在合同安排中就权利和义务达成的一致意见，与为构建安排而设立的单独主体的法律形式赋予各参与方的权利和义务是一致的，或者不矛盾。

26. 在其他情况下，各参与方使用合同安排撤销或修改为构建安排而设立的单独主体的法律形式赋予参与方的权利和义务。

应用示例
例 4 　　假定两个参与方以公司制主体的形式构造了一个合营安排。各参与方在该公司制主体中拥有 50% 的所有者权益。该公司制主体能够与其所有者分离。因此，该主体持有的资产和负债即为该公司制主体的资产和负债。在这样的情况下，通过单独主体的法律形式赋予各参与方权利和义务的评估表明，各参与方均有权获得合营安排的净资产。 　　然而，各参与方通过合同安排调整了该公司的特征，以便各参与方均按约定比例对公司制主体的资产拥有权益，对该公司制主体的负债承担义务。通过合同调整公司的特征，可能导致一项安排成为共同经营。

27. 下表对共同经营各参与方合同安排的一般条款和合营企业各参与方合同安排的一般条款进行了比较。下表提供的合同条款举例并未穷尽所有内容。

合同安排条款的评估		
	共同经营	合营企业
合同安排的条款	合同安排使合营安排的各参与方享有与安排相关资产的权利,并承担与安排相关负债的义务	合同安排使合营安排的各参与方享有对安排净资产的权利(即单独主体而非参与方,享有与安排相关资产的权利,并承担与安排相关负债的义务)
对资产的权利	合同安排约定,合营安排各参与方以约定比例(例如,按各参与方在该项安排所有者权益中的比例,或者该项安排直接分配给各参与方承担活动的比例)分享与安排相关资产的全部权益(例如,权利、权属或所有权)	合同安排约定,投入该安排的资产或合营安排后续获得的资产,均是安排的资产。各参与方对该合营安排的资产不拥有任何权益(例如,权利、权属或所有权)
对负债的义务	合同安排约定,合营安排各参与方按约定比例(例如,按各参与方在该项安排所有者权益中的比例,或者该项安排直接分配给各方承担活动的比例)分担所有的负债、义务、成本和费用	合同安排约定合营安排承担该安排的负债和义务
		合同安排约定,合营安排各参与方仅以他们在该项安排中的各自出资为限承担相应的义务,或以各方向该项安排投入的未付或新增资本为限对其各自的义务承担责任,或者以上两者之和承担相应的义务
	合同安排约定,合营安排各参与方对第三方提出的索赔权负有义务	合同安排约定,合营安排的债权人就安排的债务和义务,对任何参与方都没有追索权

续表

	合同安排条款的评估	
	共同经营	合营企业
收入、费用、损益	合同安排约定,根据各参与方对合营安排业绩的贡献分配收入和费用。例如,合同安排可能约定,根据各参与方在共同经营工厂中使用的产能分配收入和费用,这可能不同于根据他们在合营安排中的所有者权益进行的分配。在其他情况下,各参与方可能已约定按特定比例分配与安排有关的损益,例如,根据各参与方在安排中的所有者权益比例。如果各参与方享有与该安排相关的资产并承担与该安排相关的负债的义务,上述约定不影响该安排成为共同经营	合同安排约定,各参与方分担与安排活动相关的损益
担保	合营安排通常要求各参与方向第三方提供担保,这些第三方可能从合营安排获得服务或向合营安排提供融资。提供此类担保的条款或各参与方提供担保的承诺本身并不能确定该合营安排是共同经营。确定该合营安排是共同经营还是合营企业的特征是,各参与方是否对与该安排相关的负债承担义务(一些参与方可能为此提供,也可能没有提供担保)	

28. 当合同安排约定各参与方享有与该安排相关资产的权利,并承担与该安排相关负债的义务时,他们是共同经营参与方,不需要为了划分合营安排而考虑其他事实或情况(应用指南第29段至33段)。

其他事实和情况的评估

29. 如果合同安排的条款没有明确规定参与方享有与该安排相关的资产的权利并承担与该安排相关的负债的义务，参与方应考虑其他事实和情况，以评估该安排是共同经营还是合营企业。

30. 一项合营安排可能通过单独主体构造，该单独主体的法律形式将参与方和单独主体分离。参与方之间达成的合同条款可能没有明确参与方对资产和负债的权利与义务，但考虑其他事实和情况，也可以使该合营安排归类为共同经营。当其他事实和情况赋予参与方享有与安排相关的资产的权利并承担与该安排相关的负债的义务，就可以将该合营安排归类为共同经营。

31. 当一项安排的活动主要是向参与方提供产出时，这表明参与方实质上有权享受由该安排资产产生的所有经济利益。通常，该安排的参与方通过阻止该安排向第三方销售产出而确保他们获得这些产出。

32. 具有这种设计和目的的安排的影响是，该安排产生的负债实质上可由参与方通过购买产出而支付的现金流量而得以清偿。如果参与方实质上是该安排持续经营所需现金流的唯一来源，这表明参与方承担了与该安排相关的负债。

应用示例

例5

假定两个参与方以公司制主体（主体C）形式构造了一项合营安排，各方拥有公司制主体50%的所有者权益。该安排的目的是生产双方各自生产过程中所需的原材料。该安排确保双方共同经营相应的设施，以生产在数量和质量上满足双方需要的原材料。

主体C（公司制主体）活动予以实施的法律形式初步表明，主体C持有的资产和负债就是主体C的资产和负债。双方之间的合同安排没有明确各方对主体C的资产和负债的权利与义务。因此，主体C的法律形式和合同安排的条款表明，该项安排是一项合营企业。

然而，各参与方还需考虑该安排的以下方面：

- 各方同意按照50：50的比例购买主体C生产的所有产出。未经合营安排双方同意，主体C不能将任何产出出售给第三方。因为该安排的目的是向各方提供各自所需的产出，向第三方的销售预计是不经常和不重要的。
- 向各方出售产出的价格由双方共同决定，以补偿主体C发生的生产成本和管理费用。基于这种经营模式，该项安排旨在盈亏平衡的水平上经营。

从上述的实际情况来看，以下事实和情况是相关的：

- 各方购买主体 C 生产的所有产出的义务反映主体 C 完全依赖各方获得其现金流量。因此，各方有义务出资以清偿主体 C 的负债。
- 各方有权获得主体 C 生产的所有产出这一事实表明，各方正在消费并因此有权获得主体 C 资产的所有经济利益。

这些事实和情况表明该项安排是共同经营。在这些情况下，即使各方在以后的生产过程中不使用他们的产出份额，而是将这些产出份额出售给第三方，有关合营安排分类的结论也不会改变。

如果各方改变了合同安排的条款，以便该安排能够向第三方出售产出，这将导致主体 C 承担需求、存货和信用风险。在这种情况下，事实和情况的改变将要求重新评估合营安排的分类。这些事实和情况可能表明该安排是合营企业。

33. 下图反映了当通过单独主体构造合营安排时，主体对一项安排进行分类所遵循的评估程序。

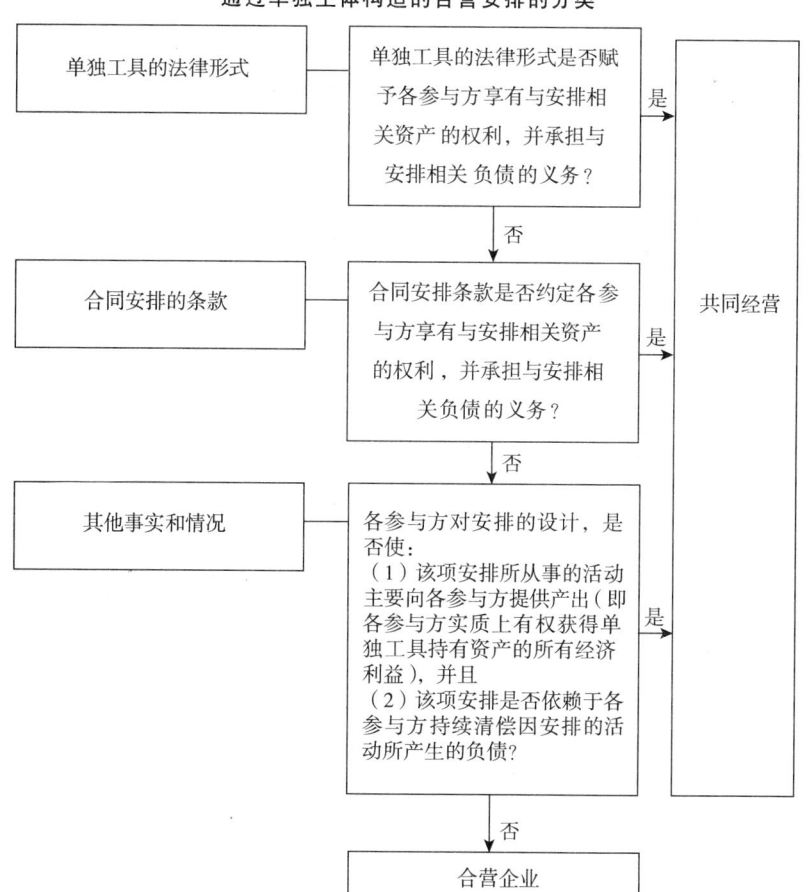

通过单独主体构造的合营安排的分类

合营安排参与方的财务报表（第 22 段）

向共同经营出售或投入资产的会计处理

34. 当作为共同经营者的主体与共同经营进行交易时，例如，出售或投入资产，这类似于主体与共同经营的其他参与方进行交易。因此，该共同经营者仅应确认交易产生的归属于共同经营中其他参与方的损益部分。

35. 当这类交易提供证据表明，向共同经营出售或投入资产的可变现净值下降或者这些资产发生减值损失，共同经营者应全额确认这些损失。

从共同经营购买资产的会计处理

36. 当作为共同经营者的主体与共同经营进行交易时，例如，购买资产，在向第三方转售资产之前，共同经营者不能确认其分享的该交易产生的损益份额。

37. 当这类交易提供证据表明购买资产的可变现净值下降或者这些资产发生减值损失，共同经营者应确认其在这些损失中的份额。

附录三　生效日期、过渡性规定和其他国际财务报告准则的撤销

本附录是本国际财务报告准则的组成部分，与本国际财务报告准则其他部分具有同等效力。

生效日期

1. 主体应自 2013 年 1 月 1 日或以后日期开始的年度期间采用本国际财务报告准则。允许提前采用。如果提前采用，主体应披露这一事实，并同时适用《国际财务报告准则第 10 号》、《国际财务报告准则第 12 号——在其他主体中权益的披露》、《国际会计准则第 27 号》（2011 年修改）和《国际会计准则第 28 号》（2011 年修改）。

1A. 2012 年 6 月发布的《合并财务报表、合营安排和在其他主体中权益的披露——过渡性规定指南》（对《国际财务报告准则第 10 号》、《国际财务报告准则第 11 号》和《国际财务报告准则第 12 号》的修改）修改了附录三第 2 段至 5 段、第 7 段至 10 段、第 12 段，新增了第 1B 段、第 12A 段和第 12B 段。主体应自 2013 年 1 月 1 日或以后日期开始的年度期间采用这些修改。如果主体提前采用《国际财务报告准则第 11 号》，主体也应提前采用这些修改。

1B. 不管《国际会计准则第 8 号——会计政策、会计估计变更和差错》第 28 段如何要求，当主体首次采用本国际财务报告准则时，主体仅需根据《国际会计准则第 8 号》第 28 段（6）的要求，列报首次采用《国际财务报告准则第 11 号》的年度期间的前一个年度期间（简称"前一个年度期间"）的定量信息。主体也可以列报当期或以前比较期间的信息，但这不是强制要求。

过渡性规定

合营企业——从比例合并转为权益法

2. 当从比例合并转为权益法时，主体应在前一个年度期间的期初确认其对合营企业的投资。初始投资应以主体以前比例合并的资产和负债的账面金额汇总数计量，

包括因合并产生的商誉。如果商誉以前属于较大的现金产出单元或一组现金产出单元,则主体应根据合营企业、所归属的现金产出单元或一组现金产出单元的相对账面金额,将商誉分配至合营企业。

3. 根据本附录第 2 段确定的投资期初余额可作为投资初始确认的认定成本。主体应将《国际会计准则第 28 号》(2011 年修改)第 40 段至 43 段的规定适用于投资的期初余额,以评估投资是否发生减值,并将减值损失确认为前一个年度期间的期初留存收益的调整。当主体因对以往进行比例合并的合营企业应用过渡性规定而确认在合营企业中的投资时,《国际会计准则第 12 号——所得税》中的第 15 段和第 24 段关于初始确认的例外规定不再适用。

4. 如果以前所有比例合并的资产和负债的汇总产生了负的净资产,则主体应评估其是否对负的净资产承担法定或推定义务,如果承担了义务,主体应确认相应的负债。如果主体认为其对负的净资产不承担法定或推定义务,主体不应确认相应的负债,但应调整列报的最早期间的期初留存收益。主体应在前一个年度期间的期初和首次采用本国际财务报告准则时,披露这一事实,及其在合营企业损失中的累积未确认份额。

5. 主体应披露在前一个年度期间期初汇总列示的投资余额中的资产和负债的明细。主体应以汇总的方式披露适用于过渡性规定第 2 段至 6 段的所有合营企业。

6. 初始确认后,主体应根据《国际会计准则第 28 号》(2011 年修改)使用权益法对其在合营企业中的投资进行会计处理。

共同经营——从权益法转为对资产和负债进行会计处理

7. 当主体对其在共同经营中的权益从权益法转为对资产和负债进行会计处理时,主体应在前一个年度期间的期初终止确认以前使用权益法进行会计处理的投资,并终止确认根据《国际会计准则第 28 号》(2011 年修改)第 38 段构成主体在安排中净投资的其他项目,同时确认主体在有关共同经营权益的各项资产和负债中的份额,包括可能构成该投资账面金额的商誉。

8. 主体应根据合同安排,以约定比例的权利和义务为基础,确定其在与共同经营相关的资产和负债中的权益份额。主体应将相关资产和负债从前一个年度期间权益法形成的投资的期初金额中予以分解后,作为相关资产和负债的期初金额。

9. 之前采用权益法进行会计处理的投资和根据《国际会计准则第 28 号》(2011 年修改)第 38 段构成主体对安排净投资的其他项目,与确认的资产和负债净额(包括商誉)之间的差额:

(1) 如果已确认的资产和负债的净额(包括商誉)大于终止确认的投资(以及构成主体净投资的其他项目),应首先抵销与投资相关的商誉,剩余部分调整前一个年度期间的期初留存收益。

(2) 如果已确认的资产和负债的净额(包括商誉)小于终止确认的投资(以及

构成主体净投资的其他项目），应调整前一个年度期间的期初留存收益。

10. 主体从权益法转为对资产和负债进行会计处理，应在前一个年度期间的期初，说明终止确认的投资、已确认资产和负债以及调整计入的期初留存收益的剩余差额之间的协调关系。

11. 当主体确认了与其在共同经营中的权益相关的资产和负债时，《国际会计准则第12号》第15段和第24段中的初始确认例外情况不适用。

主体单独财务报表中的过渡性规定

12. 之前根据《国际会计准则第27号》第10段在单独财务报表中以成本法或者根据《国际财务报告准则第9号》对其在共同经营中的权益进行会计处理主体应：

（1）终止确认该投资，并根据本附录第7段至9段确定的金额确认主体与其在共同经营中的权益相关的资产和负债。

（2）说明在列报的前一个年度期间的期初终止确认的投资、已确认资产和负债以及调整计入的期初留存收益的剩余差额之间的协调关系。

12A. 尽管在附录三第2段至12段中参照了"前一个年度期间"，主体也可以列报以前期间调整后的比较信息，但这不是强制要求。如果主体没有列报以前期间调整后的比较信息，所有对"前一个年度期间"的参照应理解为"列报调整后的最早比较期间"。

12B. 如果主体列报了以前期间未调整的比较信息，主体应明确这些信息是未经调整的，声明这些信息是在不同基础上编制的，并对该基础进行解释。

13. 当主体由于应用本附录第12段有关共同经营的过渡性规定而在其单独财务报表中确认与其在共同经营中的权益相关的资产和负债时，《国际会计准则第12号》第15段和第24段关于初始确认的例外规定不再适用。

参照《国际财务报告准则第9号》

14. 如果主体已采用本国际财务报告准则，但尚未采用《国际财务报告准则第9号》，参照《国际财务报告准则第9号》应理解为参照《国际会计准则第39号——金融工具：确认和计量》。

其他国际财务报告准则的撤销

15. 本国际财务报告准则取代了下列国际财务报告准则：
（1）《国际会计准则第31号——合营企业中的权益》；和
（2）《解释公告第13号——共同控制主体：合营者的非货币性投入》

理事会批准 2011 年 5 月发布的《国际财务报告准则第 11 号——合营安排》

国际会计准则理事会 15 位理事同意批准发布《国际财务报告准则第 11 号——合营安排》

Sir David 爵士　　　　Chairman
Stephen Cooper
Philippe Danjou
Jan Engström
Patrick Finnegan
Amaro Luiz de Oliveira Gomes
Prabhakar Kalavacherla
Elke König
Patricia McConnell
Warren J McGregor
Paul Pacter
Darrel Scott
John T Smith
Tatsumi Yamada
Wei–Guo Zhang

《国际财务报告准则第 11 号——合营安排》结论基础

国际财务报告准则第 11 号——合营安排

目 录

	段落
引言	1－3
目标	4－12
《国际会计准则第 31 号》存在的问题	7－8
根据《国际财务报告准则第 11 号》的原则改进《国际会计准则第 31 号》	9－12
范围	13－18
范围排除	15－18
合营安排	19－23
共同控制	20－23
合营安排的类型	24－37
合营安排参与方的财务报表	38－51
共同经营	38－40
合营企业	41－45
主体与其作为共同经营者的共同经营之间的交易，以及将《解释公告第 13 号》并入本国际财务报告准则	46－47
参与合营安排但不具有共同控制的参与方列报其在合营安排中的权益	48－50
持有待售的共同经营	51
披露	52－55
生效日期	56－59
过渡性规定	60－69
对《征求意见稿第 9 号》主要变动的概述	70
成本—效益分析	71－78

本结论基础与《国际财务报告准则第 11 号》一并发布，但不构成其组成部分。

引言

1. 本结论基础概述了国际会计准则理事会在制定《国际财务报告准则第 11 号——合营安排》过程中的考虑。理事会理事个人对有些因素比其他因素更为重视。

2. 理事会在议程中增加合营企业项目，是为了减少国际财务报告准则与美国公认会计原则之间的差异。《国际财务报告准则第 11 号》的规定未经美国财务会计准则委员会考量。

3. 理事会重点通过制定以原则为基础的合营安排会计处理方法并要求改进信息披露，提高主体在财务报表中对合营安排的如实列报。尽管理事会致力于改进合营安排的报告，但其结果是，与已被取代的《国际会计准则第 31 号——合营企业中的权益》相比，本国际财务报告准则与美国公认会计原则实现了进一步趋同。

目标

4. 《国际财务报告准则第 11 号》规定了主体在合营安排中的权益的确认和计量要求。主体在合营安排中的权益的披露要求已经包含在《国际财务报告准则第 12 号——在其他主体中权益的披露》（参见第 52 段至 55 段）。《国际财务报告准则第 11 号》主要解决《国际会计准则第 31 号》两方面的问题，理事会认为以下两方面问题影响了合营安排报告质量的提高：第一，安排的结构是会计处理的唯一决定因素；第二，主体对共同控制主体中权益的会计处理具有选择权。

5. 理事会没有重新考虑《国际会计准则第 31 号》的所有规定。例如，理事会没有重新考虑权益法。因此，本结论基础未讨论《国际会计准则第 31 号》中理事会没有重新考虑的规定。

6. 理事会在《征求意见稿第 9 号——合营安排》中公布了它的建议。该征求意见稿于 2007 年 9 月发布，征求意见截止期为 2008 年 1 月 11 日。理事会共收到 110 多份反馈意见函。

《国际会计准则第 31 号》存在的问题

7. 根据一项安排是否通过某一主体进行构造，《国际会计准则第 31 号》规定了不同的会计处理方法。共同控制经营和共同控制资产不需要设立独立于参与方的主体或财务结构。《国际会计准则第 31 号》要求这两类安排的参与方确认由此产生的资产、负债、收入和费用。如果安排需要设立独立的主体，《国际会计准则第 31 号》

则将其分类为共同控制主体。在共同控制主体中拥有权益的参与方可以使用比例合并法或者权益法对其进行会计处理。

8. 仅基于是否存在主体采用不同会计处理,以及对于共同控制主体具有不同的会计处理选择权,这种做法的问题在于,给予参与方类似权利和义务的安排却使用不同的会计处理方法。相反,对于给予参与方不同权利和义务的安排却使用类似的会计处理方法。理事会的政策是在任何可能的情况下排除会计准则中不同会计处理的选择权。这些选择权导致相似的交易却使用不同的会计处理方法。因此,将削弱财务信息的可比性。

根据《国际财务报告准则第 11 号》的原则改进《国际会计准则第 31 号》

9. 理事会认为合营安排的会计处理应反映参与方由于在该安排中拥有权益而享有的权利和承担的义务,而不考虑这些安排的结构和法律形式。这是《国际财务报告准则第 11 号》为合营安排参与方对其在合营安排中的权益进行会计处理而设定的原则。然而,理事会承认,在某些情况下,合营安排的结构或法律形式对确定参与方在该安排中的权利和义务的影响具有决定性作用,并因此也就决定了该合营安排的类型(参见结论基础第 26 段至 31 段)。

10. 《国际会计准则第 31 号》要求主体在对所有共同控制主体中的权益进行会计处理时,选择相同的会计处理方法(即比例合并法或权益法)。对主体在所有不同的共同控制主体中的权益采用同一种会计处理方法,可能无法如实列报主体在每一个共同控制主体中的权益。例如,主体的会计政策要求对其所有共同控制主体中的权益均采用比例合并法进行会计处理,该主体按比例合并法确认所有资产和负债,即使这样做并没有如实反映主体对特定合营安排中的资产和负债的权利和义务。相反,当主体对特定合营安排中的权利和义务的确认而使得主体确认了资产和负债时,该主体应使用权益法对其在所有共同控制主体中的权益进行会计处理。

11. 本国际财务报告准则所要求的合营安排会计处理不取决于主体会计政策的选择,而是要求主体对每一项合营安排,应用本国际财务报告准则的原则,确认由此产生的权利和义务。理事会决定,当主体对一项合营安排的资产不享有权利且对负债不承担义务时,比例合并法不是处理合营安排中权益的适当方法。相反,当主体对合营安排的资产享有权利,对债务承担义务时,权益法也不是处理合营安排中权益的适当方法。理事会认为,如果主体对其不享有权利的资产和不承担义务的负债进行确认,或对其享有权利的资产和承担义务的负债不进行确认,这都会误导财务报表的使用者。

12. 理事会重新考虑了《国际会计准则第 31 号》中对合营安排中的权益的披露要求。理事会认为,《国际财务报告准则第 12 号》中的披露要求将会使财务报表使用者更好地理解主体通过合营安排承担的经营的性质和状况。

范围

13. 本国际财务报告准则适用于合营安排的所有参与方。本国际财务报告准则未改变《国际会计准则第 31 号》所要求的安排被认定为"合营企业"的两个重要特征，一是存在制约安排各参与方的合同安排；二是合同安排要求两个或两个以上的参与方共同控制该安排。

14. 理事会认为，《国际财务报告准则第 10 号——合并财务报表》中新的控制定义和评估控制的应用规定，将有助于主体确定一项安排是被控制还是被共同控制，并且还会促使主体重新考虑其之前作出的与被投资主体之间关系的评估。尽管重新评估可能会得到不同的结果，但理事会认为，适用于《国际会计准则第 31 号》的安排，一般而言也适用于《国际财务报告准则第 11 号》。

范围排除

15. 理事会重新考虑了《国际会计准则第 31 号》的范围排除规定，这在《征求意见稿第 9 号》中有所提及。理事会决定，《征求意见稿第 9 号》中所排除的风险资本组织、共同基金、信托公司和包括投连险基金在内的类似主体持有的在合营企业中的权益，应根据《国际财务报告准则第 9 号——金融工具》以公允价值计量，且其变动计入损益，更恰当的是作为计量方面的豁免，而不是范围排除。

16. 理事会观察到，当认定风险资本组织、共同基金、信托公司或包括投连险基金在内的类似主体在合营安排中拥有权益时，这是因为该安排具有《国际财务报告准则第 11 号》描述的合营安排的特征（即存在两个或两个以上的参与方共同控制一项安排的合同安排）。

17. 理事会还观察到，《征求意见稿第 9 号》的范围排除并非是因为这些安排不具有合营安排特征，而是对风险资本组织、共同基金、信托公司或包括投连险基金在内的类似主体所持有的投资以公允价值计量比应用权益法能够为财务报表使用者提供更有用的信息。

18. 因此，理事会决定保留选择权，允许主体根据《国际财务报告准则第 9 号》以公允价值计量其在合营企业中的权益，并将公允价值变动计入损益。但理事会声明，这是对主体使用权益法计量其在合营企业中权益的要求的豁免，而不是将这些主体拥有权益的合营企业中排除在《国际财务报告准则第 11 号》的范围之外。

合营安排

19. 理事会决定使用术语"合营安排",而不是"合营企业",来描述本国际财务报告准则规定的安排。正如结论基础第 13 段所提到的,本国际财务报告准则未改变《国际会计准则第 31 号》所要求的合营安排成为"合营企业"的两个重要特征:一是存在制约安排各参与方的合同安排;二是合同安排要求两个或两个以上的参与方共同控制该安排。

共同控制

20. 在《征求意见稿第 9 号》中提出的"合营安排"的定义,要求该安排的所有参与方"分享决策权"。一些意见反馈者质疑,如何实现"分享决策权",并且如何区分其与"共同控制"。理事会在征求意见稿中引入"分享决策权"这个术语,而不是"共同控制",是因为在《国际会计准则第 27 号——合并财务报表和单独财务报表》中已经对控制进行了定义,控制是指统驭另一主体的财务和经营政策的权力①。在对《征求意见稿第 9 号》重新考虑过程中,理事会决定,在合营安排中,正是参与方所从事的活动才是参与方分享控制权或决策权的分项,而无论这项活动是否由一个单独的主体进行。因此,理事会决定,"共同控制"这个术语比"分享决策权"更好地表达了合营安排的主旨,即进行共同控制的参与方之间共同享有的情况。

21. 理事会没有重新考虑《国际会计准则第 31 号》或《征求意见稿第 9 号》中定义的"共同控制"概念(即使参与方控制一项安排的决策要求所有参与方一致同意)。然而,本国际财务报告准则中的"共同控制"定义不同于《国际会计准则第 31 号》或《征求意见稿第 9 号》中的定义。变动的原因是为了使"共同控制"的定义与《国际财务报告准则第 10 号》中"控制"的定义相一致。《国际财务报告准则第 11 号》指出,根据《国际财务报告准则第 10 号》的控制定义和相应指南,安排的参与方首先应评估所有参与方或一组参与方是否集体控制该安排。一旦主体认为安排由所有参与方或一组参与方集体控制,则仅当显著影响该安排收益的经济活动(即相关活动)的决策需要这些集体控制的参与方一致同意时才存在共同控制。

22. 一些意见反馈者提出,与《国际会计准则第 31 号》不同,《征求意见稿第 9 号》中没有包括"合营安排中的投资者"这个术语,理事会在对《征求意见稿第 9 号》重新考虑过程中对此予以澄清,并不需要合营安排的所有参与方都拥有共同控制才使得该安排成为合营安排。实际上,一些参与方拥有共同控制的权利,而另一些

---

① 《国际会计准则第 27 号》中合并财务报表的要求被 2011 年发布的《国际财务报告准则第 10 号——合并财务报表》所取代,并且控制的定义被修订。

参与方虽然能够参与这项合营安排，但是他们没有共同控制这项安排的权利。理事会决定使用"共同经营者"这一术语表示那些对"共同经营"具有共同控制权利的参与方，使用"合营者"这一术语表示对"合营企业"具有共同控制权利的参与方（参见结论基础第24段）。

23. 理事会观察到，合营安排的参与方可能会随时变更或调整该安排的治理和决策程序。作为这种变动的结果，某些参与方可能获得或失去对该项安排的共同控制。因此，理事会决定，如果事实和情况发生了变化，合营安排的各参与方应重新评估他们是否还拥有对该项安排的共同控制权。

合营安排的类型

24. 本国际财务报告准则将合营安排分成"共同经营"和"合营企业"两类。对共同经营具有共同控制的参与方（"共同经营者"）享有与该项安排相关资产的权利，并承担与该安排相关负债的义务，而对合营企业具有共同控制的参与方（"合营者"）享有该项安排净资产的权利。

25. 理事会在重新考虑《征求意见稿第9号》的过程中决定将合营安排分成两类。《征求意见稿第9号》原来建议将合营安排分成三类，"共同经营"、"共同资产"和"合营企业"。理事会观察到，在一些情况下，难以评估一项安排是"共同经营"还是"共同资产"。因为这两类合营安排的要素有时都会出现（在许多安排中，共同资产也都是共同经营的。因此，这类安排可以被归类为"共同资产"，也可以被归类为"共同经营"）。此外，这两类合营安排的会计处理结果是一样的（即确认资产、负债以及相应的收入和费用）。基于上述原因，理事会决定将"共同经营"和"共同资产"合并为一类合营安排，称为"共同经营"。这个决定使本国际财务报告准则对合营安排的两种分类与两种可能的会计处理结果（即确认资产、负债、收入和费用，或者使用权益法对一项投资进行确认）（即"共同经营"和"合营企业"）相一致，简化了本国际财务报告准则。

26. 理事会观察到，当参与方未通过设立一个独立工具来构造合营安排时，（即这类安排是《国际会计准则第31号》中的"共同控制经营"和"共同控制资产"），这些参与方确认他们在该合同安排中享有与该项安排相关资产的权利，并承担与该安排相关负债的义务。这样的安排就是共同经营。

27. 在形成上述决定时，理事会承认一项未通过设立独立工具的合营安排的参与方有可能设定了一些合同安排条款，使得这些参与方仅享有该项安排净资产的权利。理事会认为，这样的可能性很小，并且当合营安排未通过独立工具进行构造时，对合营安排分类引入额外评估的收益将无法弥补因本国际财务报告准则复杂性所增加的成本。这是因为在绝大多数情况下，未通过独立工具构造的合营安排以总额为基础的会计处理上可以如实地反映参与方在这些安排中的权利和义务。

28. 理事会承认,将《国际会计准则第31号》中共同控制主体分类为本国际财务报告准则的共同经营和合营企业,需要主体运用职业判断,评估其在这些安排中的权利和义务。

29. 理事会考虑了《国际财务报告准则第3号——企业合并》中定义的"业务"是否有助于区分合营企业和共同经营。由于所有类型的合营安排均包含"业务"特征,因而理事会决定不采用这种方法。

30. 理事会还决定,不应认为是通过独立工具所构造的一项安排就是合营企业是一个不可推翻的假定。理事会决定,通过设立独立工具来运行合营安排的各参与方应根据所有事实和情况对该安排进行评估。理事会指出,主体应考虑独立工具的法律形式、合同安排条款以及其他相关的事实和情况。

31. 在使用这种方法时,理事会观察到,独立工具的法律形式提供了参与方享有与该项安排相关资产的权利,并承担与该安排相关负债的义务的最初标志。当独立工具的法律形式不能区分参与方和该工具时,应当作为例外。在这种情况下,理事会决定,对该独立工具赋予参与方的权利和义务进行评估将足以判断该安排是否是共同经营。

32. 理事会认为,在许多情况下,特定法律形式的选择是由该特定法律形式传递的内在的经济实质所决定。然而,理事会观察到,在一些情况下,特定法律形式的选择受到税收、监管要求或其他因素的影响,这些因素能够改变参与方最初欲获得的内在的经济实质。在这些情况下,参与方可能会使用其合同安排对法律形式影响其权利和义务进行调整。

33. 理事会指出,其他事实和情况可能也会影响合营安排参与方的权利和义务,最终会影响该安排的分类。因此,如果参与方设计该安排旨在为参与方提供产出(即参与方有权获得与该安排相关资产的所有经济利益),作为该安排设计的结果,参与方也承担与该安排相关负债的义务,则参与方应确认与该安排相关的资产和负债。

34. 本国际财务报告准则将"合营企业"定义为,共同控制一项安排的参与方(即合营者)对其净资产享有权利的安排。理事会观察到,在合营企业定义中使用"净资产"术语旨在描述合营者拥有在该安排中的投资。然而,这一定义(即"享有合营安排净资产的权利")也不妨碍合营者因涉入合营企业而承担的净负债。例如,当合营企业发生的损失导致合营者的投资减记至零后,因合营者为合营企业可能发生的损失提供了担保而有义务承担其投资损失。理事会观察到,无论合营者提供的担保,还是其在合营企业发生损失时需要承担的负债,均不能决定该安排是共同经营。

35. 《征求意见稿第9号》的许多意见反馈者担心,合营企业可能仅是"剩余项"。因为这些反馈者认为合营企业意味着,在参与方已对单项资产的权利或者对费用或筹资的义务确认后,合营企业仅是该安排的剩余资产和负债。为回应这些担忧,理事会澄清,合营安排的计量单元是两个或两个以上的参与方共同控制的一项经济活动,并且任何一个参与方应评估其享有的与该经济活动相关资产的权利,并承担的与该经济活动相关负债的义务。因此,"合营企业"术语指参与方拥有投资的一项共同控制活动。

36. 在重新考虑《征求意见稿第 9 号》过程中,理事会阐明,不同的合营安排或不同类型的合营安排能够在处理诸如相关联的不同经济活动的同一安排或框架协议下建立。理事会还观察到,在同一个单独主体中,参与方可以进行不同的经济活动,享有与不同经济活动相关的资产的权利,并承担与不同经济活动相关的负债的义务,使得在同一个单独主体中产生不同的合营安排类型。然而,理事会承认,尽管这种情况从原理上讲可能存在,但实务中很少见。

37. 理事会观察到,合营安排参与方的权利和义务会随着时间发生变化。例如,合营安排目的的变动可能会引起对合同安排条款的重新考虑。因此,理事会决定,应当根据事实和情况的变化,对合营安排的类型进行持续评估。

合营安排参与方的财务报表

共同经营

38. 关于参与方在合营安排权益中的会计处理,《征求意见稿第 9 号》的一些意见反馈者询问,比例合并法与确认共同经营产生的资产、负债、收入和费用(或其份额)之间有何差异。理事会指出,比例合并法与确认共同经营产生的资产、负债、收入和费用(或其份额)之间存在两个主要差异。第一个差异是,如合同安排中规定的,参与方对共同经营中相关资产、负债、收入和费用的权利和义务可能与其在共同经营中所享有的所有者权益不同。本国际财务报告准则要求在共同经营中拥有权益的参与方根据合同安排中约定的参与方在共同经营资产、负债、收入和费用中的份额确认相应的资产、负债、收入和费用,而不是根据其在共同经营中所拥有的所有者权益确认相应的资产、负债、收入和费用。与比例合并法的第二个差异是,参与方需要在单独财务报表中确认其在共同经营中的权益。因此,参与方单独财务报表所确认的与参与方合并财务报表或使用权益法对投资进行会计处理的财务报表之间将没有差异。

39. 意见反馈者还建议,本国际财务报告准则应进一步明确对共同经营中资产份额会计处理的要求。《征求意见稿第 9 号》的许多意见反馈者并不清楚,享有资产权利的共同经营的参与方是应确认"使用权"或对份额的,或是应直接"根据资产属性的分类确认共同资产的份额"。这些不确定性产生于对准则的不同解释,即对权利的会计处理,还是对资产份额的会计处理。理事会决定,共同经营的参与方应根据适用于特定资产的国际财务报告准则确认其资产或者资产份额。

40. 《征求意见稿第 9 号》的一些意见反馈者提出另一种担心,对于共同经营参与方的会计处理而言,应当如何描述与资产和负债份额相关的计量单元。理事会观察到,《征求意见稿第 9 号》并不想改变《国际会计准则第 31 号》在这方面的规定,在《国际会计准则第 31 号》中"份额"由合同安排所决定。理事会决定,合同安排基本上不仅描述了共同经营参与方对资产和负债的"份额"或"部分",而且也描述了共同经营产生的收入和费用的"份额"。

合营企业

41. 关于合营企业中权益的会计处理,理事会决定,主体应根据《国际会计准则第 28 号——在联营企业和合营企业中的投资》使用权益法确认其在合营企业中的权益,除非根据《国际会计准则第 28 号》主体被豁免应用权益法的。理事会在作出该决定时考虑了《征求意见稿第 9 号》的一些意见反馈者的意见,这些反馈者提出共同控制和重大影响是不同的。持有上述观点的反馈者认为,使用同一种方法,即权益法,对联营和合营企业进行会计处理是不恰当的。尽管理事会承认重大影响和共同控制是不同的,但理事会决定,除《国际会计准则第 28 号》(2011 年修改)中描述的特定情况外,权益法是对合营企业进行会计处理的最优方法,因为它是一种核算主体在被投资方净资产中权益的会计处理方法。对权益法的重新考虑不属于合营企业项目的范围。

42. 其他意见反馈者对取消比例合并法表示担忧。这些反馈者认为,比例合并法更如实地反映了合营安排的经济实质,并且更符合财务报表使用者的信息需求。理事会承认这些担忧,但是观察到,本国际财务报告准则使用的方法与其就构成主体在合营安排中权益的经济实质的观点是一致的,这种观点与这些反馈者的观点是不同的。有证据表明,对共同控制主体中权益的会计处理,将近一半的主体采用比例合并法,一半使用权益法。由于《国际会计准则第 31 号》赋予主体的会计处理选择权引起的实务方面的差异,是制定《国际财务报告准则第 11 号》的主要动因(参见结论基础第 7 段和第 8 段)。这种差异不可避免地将成为分歧的根源。

43. 理事会认为,对合营安排的会计处理应如实地反映参与方在该安排中的资产和负债方面的权利和义务。在这一方面,理事会观察到,不同合营安排的经济活动可能在运作上非常相似,但这些合营安排参与方同意的合同条款却赋予参与方与这些活动相关的资产和负债的不同权利和义务。因此,理事会认为,这些安排的经济实质并不完全取决于通过合营安排进行的活动是否与参与方自身进行的活动密切相关,或者参与方是否密切参与这些安排的经营。相反,这些安排的经济实质取决于参与方从事这些活动时所能获取的权利和承担的义务。在对合营安排的会计处理中应当如实地反映这些权利和义务。

44. 理事会观察到,本国际财务报告准则要求当合同安排规定了参与方享有资产的权利和承担负债的义务时,参与方应对这些资产和负债进行会计处理。理事会认为,基于本国际财务报告准则的原则对合营安排进行会计处理,不仅有助于如实地反映主体在合营安排中的权益,而且有助于增强可比性。因为对于参与方享有资产的权利和承担负债的义务的所有这类安排,将采用相同的会计处理。同样,对于参与方对净资产享有权利的安排,也将采用相同的会计处理。

45. 理事会认为,取消比例合并法不会减少财务报表使用者的信息量。这是因为与《国际会计准则第 31 号》相比,《国际财务报告准则第 12 号》中关于主体在合营企业中的权益的披露要求,更能提高信息质量。当合营企业对于报告主体而言很重要时,《国际财务报告准则第 12 号》中的披露要求将提供给使用者关于单个合营企业的相关信息。此外,理事会指出,《国际财务报告准则第 12 号》中汇总的财务信息比《国际会计准则第 31 号》的财务信息更详细,这些信息为使用者评估通过合营企业进行的活动对报告主体的影响提供了更好的基础。

主体与其作为共同经营者的共同经营之间的交易,以及将《解释公告第 13 号》并入本国际财务报告准则

46. 在重新审议《征求意见稿第 9 号》时,理事会注意到,征求意见稿没有考虑主体与其作为共同经营者的共同经营之间的交易的会计处理。理事会观察到,本国际财务报告准则并不希望改变主体根据《国际会计准则第 31 号》对此类交易进行处理的会计程序,但承认本国际财务报告准则应明确这些规定是什么。

47. 理事会还决定将合营者与合营企业之间进行交易的会计处理规定收入《国际会计准则第 28 号》(2011 年修改),包括《解释公告第 13 号——共同控制主体:合营者的非货币性投入》的一致意见。

参与合营安排但不具有共同控制的参与方列报其在合营安排中的权益

48. 理事会决定在本国际财务报告准则中明确,即使并非所有参与方对一项安排具有共同控制,该安排也可能是合营安排。这与《国际会计准则第 31 号》是一致的,该准则将"合营企业中的投资者"定义为"参与合营企业但不具有共同控制的参与方"。然而,理事会注意到,将术语"投资者"特指对安排没有共同控制的参与方,可能会引起困惑,因为共同控制该安排的参与方也是这些安排的投资者。因此,理事会对本国际财务报告准则的用词进行了修改,以避免这种困惑。然而,尽管理事会在重新审议《征求意见稿第 9 号》时强调,本国际财务报告准则针对共同控制一项合营安排的参与方制定了确认和计量的规定,但理事会决定解决对参与合营安排但不具有共同控制的参与方的会计处理规定,以减少实务中的分歧。

49. 对于参与共同经营但不具有共同控制的参与方,理事会重点讨论了那些合同安排明确规定其享有与共同经营相关资产的权利并承担与共同经营相关负债的义务的参与方。理事会得出结论,尽管这些参与方不是共同经营者,但他们确实对与共同经营相关的资产、负债、收入和费用拥有权利和义务,因此,他们应根据合同安排的条款对其予以确认。

50. 理事会考虑到,《国际会计准则第 31 号》对这些参与合营企业但不具有共同控制的参与方的会计处理规定是恰当的,因而决定在本国际财务报告准则中继续予以执行。所以,这样的参与方应根据《国际财务报告准则第 9 号》对其投资进行会计处理,或者如果参与方对合营企业具有重大影响,则应当根据《国际会计准则第 28 号》(2011 年修改)进行会计处理。

持有待售的共同经营

51.《征求意见稿第 9 号》没有规定主体应当如何对被分类为持有待售共同经营中的权益进行会计处理。理事会决定,共同经营者应根据《国际财务报告准第 5 号——持有待售的非流动资产和终止经营》对被分类为持有待售共同经营中的权益进行会计处理。理事会还明确,《国际财务报告准第 5 号》中关于将资产处置组分类为持有待售的也适用于被分类为持有待售共同经营中的权益。

披露

52. 作为对《征求意见稿第 9 号》和《征求意见稿第 10 号——合并财务报表》重新审议的一部分,理事会找到了一个时机,对子公司、合营安排、联营企业以及未纳入合并财务报表范围的结构化主体的披露要求进行整合并使保持一致,并将在一个单独的国际财务报告准则中列示这些要求。

53. 理事会注意到,《国际会计准则第 27 号》(2003 年修订)、《国际会计准则第 28 号》(2003 年修订)和《国际会计准则第 31 号》包含了许多相似的披露要求。《征求意见稿第 9 号》已经提出了对联营企业和合营企业的披露要求进行修改,以使得这两类投资的披露要求更为接近。理事会指出,绝大多数反馈意见者同意《征求意见稿第 9 号》提出的建议,使合营企业的披露与《国际会计准则第 28 号》中对联营企业的披露更为接近。

54. 因此,理事会将在子公司、合营安排、联营企业以及未纳入合并财务报表范围的结构化主体中的权益的披露要求都列入一个单独的综合性准则,即《国际财务报告准则第 12 号》。

55. 与《国际财务报告准则第 12 号》一并发布的结论基础概述了理事会制定该准则时的考虑,包括对《征求意见稿第 9 号》中披露建议的反馈意见的审议。因此,《国际财务报告准则第 11 号》没有包含披露要求,并且本结论基础没有包括理事会对《征求意见稿第 9 号》披露要求建议的反馈意见的考虑。

生效日期

56. 理事会决定使本国际财务报告准则的生效日期与《国际财务报告准则第10号》、《国际财务报告准则第12号》、《国际会计准则第27号——单独财务报表》和《国际会计准则第28号》（2011年修改）的生效日期保持一致。在作出该决定时，理事会注意到，上述这五项国际财务报告准则都与报告主体与其他主体间特定关系（即当报告主体对另一主体具有控制、共同控制或重大影响）的评估、相关会计处理和披露要求有关。因此，理事会得出结论，单独应用《国际财务报告准则第11号》而不应用其他四项国际财务报告准则可能引起不必要的困惑。

57. 理事会通常将生效日期定在一项国际财务报告准则发布后的12至18个月间。当为那些国际财务报告准则决定生效日期时，理事会考虑了以下因素：

（1）许多国家翻译准则并将强制性要求纳入法律所需的时间。

（2）合并财务报表项目与2007年开始的全球金融危机相关，为响应二十国集团领导人、金融稳定理事会、财务报表使用者、监管机构和其他利益相关方的迫切要求，理事会加快了其进程，以提高主体表外经济活动的会计处理和披露。

（3）收到的反馈意见者对2010年10月发布的《意见征询——生效日期和过渡性规定》反馈的评论。该《意见征询》针对2011年发布的国际财务报告准则的实施成本、生效日期和过渡性规定。大多数反馈意见者不认为合并财务报表和合营安排的国际财务报告准则在其实施所需的时间和资源方面有较大影响。此外，只有少数意见反馈者认为，这些国际财务报告准则的生效日期应与2011年发布的其他国际财务报告准则的生效日期保持一致。

58. 考虑到这些因素，理事会决定要求主体在2013年1月1日或以后日期开始的年度期间采用这五项国际财务报告准则。

59. 《意见征询》的大多数反馈意见者支持提前采用2011年发布的这五项国际财务报告准则。反馈意见者强调，提前采用对于2011年和2012年的国际财务报告准则首次采用者尤其重要。理事会接受了这些意见，并基于结论基础第56段指出的使理事会决定为这五项国际财务报告准则设定同一个生效日期的原因，决定只有在主体同时应用其他国际财务报告准则（《国际财务报告准则第10号》、《国际财务报告准则第12号》、《国际会计准则第27号》（2011年修改）和《国际会计准则第28号》（2011年修改））时才允许提前采用《国际财务报告准则第11号》，以避免降低财务报表的可比性。尽管主体应同时应用这五项国际财务报告准则，理事会注意到，如果主体提前提供《国际财务报告准则第12号》所要求的信息有助于使用者更好地理解主体与其他主体关系的话，主体也可以提前提供《国际财务报告准则第12号》要求的信息。

过渡性规定

60. 征求意见稿建议对这些规定进行追溯调整。理事会在重新审议《征求意见稿第 9 号》时注意到,受本国际财务报告准则变动影响的主体将拥有充足的时间对这些规定进行追溯调整。理事会了解到一些主体根据他们对《征求意见稿第 9 号》建议的分析,利用《国际会计准则第 31 号》对共同控制主体提供的会计处理选择权,已经对合营安排中的权益的会计处理进行了追溯调整。

61. 然而在讨论中,理事会考虑了《征求意见稿第 9 号》的一些反馈意见者关心的问题,这些反馈者担心追溯调整相关规定将耗费过多的成本和精力。对于这种担心,理事会决定,在从比例合并法到权益法变动的情况下,主体不应对这两种方法会计处理的差异进行追溯调整,而应在最早列报期间的期初将之前使用比例合并法列示的资产和负债的账面金额,包括任何由于并购产生的商誉,予以汇总,作为一项投资。

62. 理事会还决定,主体应根据《国际会计准则第 28 号》(2011 年修改)的第 40 段至 43 段对投资的期初金额进行减值测试,并用减值损失调整列报的最早期间的期初留存收益。

63. 理事会还考虑了以前使用比例合并法的安排在向权益法过渡时产生负的净资产的情况。在这种情况下,主体应当评估其是否承担与负的净资产相关的法定或推定义务。理事会得出结论,如果主体不对负的净资产承担法定或推定义务,就不应确认相应的负债,但需要调整列报的最早期间的期初留存收益。应要求主体披露其在列报的最早期间的期初和首次采用国际财务报告准则日对合营企业损失累积未确认部分的事实和金额。

64. 理事会还考虑了这些披露要求,以帮助财务报表使用者理解合营安排会计处理方法从比例合并法转变为权益法的影响。为满足这一需求,理事会决定主体应披露在列报的最早期间的期初已经汇总列示的投资金额中的资产和负债的明细。

65. 理事会重新审议了主体对其在共同经营中的权益从权益法转变为对资产和负债进行会计处理的过渡性规定。理事会决定,要求主体基于应用权益法时所使用的信息,确认与其在共同经营中的权益相关的每一项资产(包括购并产生的商誉)和负债的账面金额,而不是要求该主体在过渡日重新计量其在资产和负债中的份额。理事会不认为要求主体因会计处理方法改变而对共同经营中资产和负债重新计量的成本会超过获得的收益。

66. 理事会注意到,主体对其在共同经营中的权益从权益法转为对资产和负债进行会计处理,会导致确认的资产和负债净额高于或低于被终止确认的投资(以及在该安排中构成主体净投资的其他项目)的金额。对于第一种情况,理事会指出,如果主体以前对这项投资计提了减值,确认的资产和负债会高于终止确认的投资。理事会注意到，根据《国际会计准则第 28 号》（2011 年修改），这样的减值损失不会分配到任何构成投资账面金额一部分的资产，包括商誉。因此，这些资产和负债的净额可能会高于这项投资的账面金额。为解决这个问题，理事会作出决定，在这种情况下，主体应首先抵销与投资相关的商誉，任何剩余差异调整列报的最早期间的期初留存收益。对于第二种情况，理事会指出，确认的资产和负债会低于终止确认投资的账面金额，例如，主体在使用权益法确定其投资的账面金额时，对被投资者的所有资产和负债使用同样的权益比例。然而，当该投资被作为共同经营进行会计处理时，主体对于其中的部分资产可能拥有较低的权益。理事会决定，在这种情况下，主体应将确认的资产和负债的净额与终止确认的投资（以及在该安排中构成主体净投资的其他项目）之间的差额调整列报的最早期间的期初留存收益。

67. 理事会还重新审议了，当主体之前以成本法或根据《国际财务报告准则第 9 号》对其在共同经营中的权益进行会计处理时，其在单独财务报表中对这部分权益进行会计处理的过渡性规定。正如结论基础第 38 段所言，理事会注意到，参与方在共同经营中的权益在其单独财务报表中的确认，不会导致参与方在单独财务报表和合并财务报表中的确认有所差异。理事会决定，主体应在列报的最早期间的期初将终止确认的投资与已确认的资产和负债之间的差额调整计入期初留存收益。

68. 理事会还考虑了披露要求，以帮助财务报表使用者理解合营安排会计处理方法从权益法转变为对资产和负债核算的经济后果，以及当主体以前对该权益以成本法或根据《国际财务报告准则第 9 号》对其在共同经营中的权益进行会计处理时，其在单独财务报表对这部分权益的会计处理。理事会决定，在这两种情况下，主体应在列报的最早期间提供终止确认的投资与分开确认的资产和负债之间的调整，并以任何剩余差异留存收益。

69. 正如结论基础第 57 段所言，《意见征询》的反馈意见者也对 2011 年发布的国际财务报告准则的过渡性规定进行了评论。关于合并财务报表和合营安排国际财务报告准则的过渡性规定，理事会指出，《意见征询》的大多数反馈意见者同意理事会之前在对这些国际财务报告准则的过渡性规定进行咨询时作出的暂时性决定。

69A. 2012 年 6 月，理事会修改了《国际财务报告准则第 10 号——合并财务报表》附录三中的过渡性规定指南。在做这些修改时，理事会决定将这些要求限定于列报《国际财务报告准则第 10 号》首次采用日前一个年度期间的调整后的比较信息。这与《国际会计准则第 1 号——财务报表列报》中包含的最低比较披露要求是一致的，《国际财务报告准则 2009－2011 的年度改进》（2012 年 5 月发布）对《国际会计准则第 1 号》作了修改。这些修改强调，当主体追溯采用一项变动的会计政策，主体至少应列报三张财务状况表（即，对于报告日为每年 12 月 31 日的主体，2012 年 1 月 1 日、2012 年 12 月 31 日和 2013 年 12 月 31 日的财务状况表）以及两张利润表和两张现金流量表（《国际会计准则第 1 号》第 40A 段和第 40B 段）。不管该要求如何规定，理事会强调，不禁止主体列报以前期间调整后的比较信息。理事会还决定对本国际财务报告准则和《国际财务报告准则第 12 号——在其他主体中权益的披露》两项准则附录三的过渡性规定指南进行类似修改。理事会注意到，如果不调整所有比较期间，那么应当要求主体声明这些事实，明确这些信息是未调整的，并解释编制这些信息的基础。

69B. 理事会还考虑了《国际会计准则第8号——会计政策、会计估计变更和差错》的披露要求。在开始应用一项国际财务报告准则时，《国际会计准则第8号》第28段（6）要求主体披露当前期间和列报的每一个以前期间，财务报表中每一项受影响项目的调整金额。当转换执行《国际财务报告准则第11号》时，对合营安排会计处理的变化有可能影响财务报表中的许多项目。理事会认为该要求对财务报表编制者而言负担较重，并同意将合营安排会计处理变化的定量影响的披露，仅限于采用《国际财务报告准则第11号》首个年度期间的前一个年度期间。

发布的《合并财务报表、合营安排和在其他主体中权益的披露——过渡性规定指南》（对《国际财务报告准则第10号》、《国际财务报告准则第11号》和《国际财务报告准则第12号》的修改）修改了附录三第2段至5段、第7段至10段、第12段，新增了第1B段、第12A段和第12B段。主体应自2013年1月1日或以后日期开始的年度期间采用这些修改。如果主体提前采用《国际财务报告准则第11号》，主体也应提前采用这些修改。主体也可以列报当期或以前比较期间的信息，但这不是强制要求。

对《征求意见稿第9号》主要变动的概述

70.《征求意见稿第9号》主要变动是：

（1）《国际财务报告准则第11号》适用于在合营安排中拥有权益的所有主体。在征求意见稿中对风险资本组织、共同基金、信托公司或包括投连险基金在内的类似主体的范围排除已经被删除，而被重新定性为对合营企业中的投资以权益法计量要求的豁免。

（2）《国际财务报告准则第11号》使用"共同控制"这一术语替代了《征求意见稿第9号》中引入的"共享决策"术语。正如《国际会计准则第31号》规定，"共同控制"是定义"合营安排"的特征之一，此外存在合同安排也是特征之一。

（3）《国际财务报告准则第11号》将合营安排分为两类——"共同经营"和"合营企业"。每一类合营安排都有特定的会计处理要求。《征求意见稿第9号》将合营安排分为三类——"共同经营"、"共同资产"和"合营企业"。

（4）《国际财务报告准则第11号》提供了应用要求，以帮助主体对其合营安排进行分类。本国际财务报告准则要求主体通过考虑其在合营安排中的权利和义务来确定该合营安排的类型。尤其是，本国际财务报告准则要求主体考虑该安排的结构和法律形式、参与方在合同安排中同意的条款以及其他相关的事实和情况。

（5）《国际财务报告准则第11号》明确，对于一项合营安排，并不是所有参与方都拥有共同控制,才使该安排成为合营安排。因此,一项合营安排的部分参与方可能仅参与该合营安排,但没有对该安排的共同控制。

(6)《解释公告第13号》的一致意见都已纳入《国际会计准则第28号》(2011年修改),相应地《解释公告第13号》被撤销。《征求意见稿第9号》建议将《解释公告第13号》的一致意见纳入合营安排准则。

(7)相关披露要求已被纳入《国际财务报告准则第12号》。《征求意见稿第9号》建议将对合营安排的披露要求纳入合营安排准则。

(8)《国际财务报告准则第11号》并未要求主体对合营企业进行会计处理从比例合并法转为权益法时,对比例合并法与权益法之间的差异进行追溯调整。相反,《国际财务报告准则第11号》要求主体在列报的最早期间的期初确认在合营企业中的投资,以主体以前按比例合并的资产(包括购并产生的商誉)和负债账面金额的汇总数进行计量。《征求意见稿第9号》建议对这些规定采用追溯调整。

成本—效益分析

71. 通用目的财务报告的目标是提供报告主体的财务信息,这些信息有助于现有和潜在的投资者、债权人和其他借款方对是否向主体提供资源作出决策。为实现这个目标,理事会致力于确保国际财务报告准则满足重大需求,并确保产生信息的整体效益高于提供这些信息的成本。虽然执行一项新国际财务报告准则的成本可能不是均匀发生的,但财务报表使用者能从财务报表的改进中获益,最终有助于资本市场和信贷市场的运行和经济资源的有效配置。

72. 成本和效益的分析必定是主观的。在做判断时,理事会考虑了以下因素:

(1)财务报表编制者发生的成本;

(2)财务报表使用者在不能获得信息时发生的成本;

(3)相比较财务报表使用者得到替代信息发生的成本,财务报表编制者提供这些信息的相对优势;

(4)由于改进财务报表而有助于作出更好的经济决策获得的效益;

(5)财务报表使用者、财务报表编制者和其他利益相关方的转换成本。

73. 理事会得出结论,本国际财务报告准则有利于财务报表的编制者和使用者。这是因为本国际财务报告准则中合营安排的会计处理遵循了原则导向的方法。这种方法使理事会删除了《国际会计准则第31号》中会计处理的选择权。因此,每一种合营安排(即"共同经营"和"合营企业")都在同一基础上进行会计处理。这有助于提高主体财务报表中合营安排信息的可验证性、可比性和可理解性。

74. 在本国际财务报告准则中,合营安排的会计处理取决于该安排产生的权利和义务(并不完全取决于参与方是否选择了特定的结构和法律形式组织其安排,也不完全取决于会计政策——比例合并法或权益法的一致采用)。因此,本国际财务报准则通过对不同合营安排运用相同的方法，促进了可比性。

75. 理事会认为，基于本国际财务报告准则列示的原则的会计处理，提高了信息的可验证性、可比性和可理解性，这有利于财务报表的编制者和使用者。首先，可验证性和可理解性的提高是因为会计处理更如实地反映了其意图披露的经济现象（即主体因该安排而拥有的权利和承担的义务），这使得编制者和使用者能更好地理解。其次，要求对每一类合营安排采用同一种会计处理将使主体对合营安排的会计处理保持一致：赋予参与方资产权利和负债义务的安排是共同经营，赋予参与方净资产权利的安排是合营企业。对合营安排进行会计处理的一致性将有助于实现财务报表之间的可比性，这有助于使用者识别和理解不同安排之间的相似之处和差异。

76. 理事会指出，财务报表编制者在对安排应用本国际财务报告准则时必须承担的成本集中于对合营安排类型的评估，而不是对该安排的会计处理。这是因为主体应用《国际会计准则第31号》对合营安排进行会计处理时，并未被要求根据该安排产生的权利和义务对这些安排予以分类，而是基于这些安排是否通过一个主体进行构造。当合营安排是通过单独主体构造时，本国际财务报告准则要求主体评估他们参与的合营安排的类型。即使对合营安排的分类是《国际会计准则第31号》所没有要求的额外评估，有助于编制者对合营安排分类的本国际财务报告准则的指南规定也不是过于复杂。理事会不认为本国际财务报告准则对合营安排分类所要求的额外评估会导致编制者发生过多的成本。

77. 理事会指出，本国际财务报告准则与征求意见稿相比，通过使合营安排类型与其会计处理相符而简化了征求意见稿的有关建议。理事会决定，一旦主体决定了该安排的分类，对该安排的会计处理将遵循本国际财务报告准则并未改变的会计处理程序（即主体将对资产和负债进行会计处理，或使用权益法对其投资进行会计处理）。然而，理事会承认，规定在合并财务报表与单独财务报表中对共同经营采用相同的会计处理方法，可能使那些被要求根据国际财务报告准则提供单独财务报表的国家或地区的主体增加成本。这是因为这些要求可能会使主体进行额外的人工操作，如，法定报表与纳税申报表的调节，并有可能要求主体向其债权人等提供变动影响的额外解释。根据本国际财务报告准则的相关规定，除了这些成本和任何其他过渡所要求的成本，一旦主体确定了合营安排类型，则对合营安排会计处理的成本会保持不变。

78. 理事会得出结论，可验证性、可比性和可理解性的提高使得主体财务报表更如实地反映其参与的合营安排，并且执行本国际财务报告准则获得的收益将超过财务报表编制者可能发生的相关成本。

《国际财务报告准则第 11 号——合营安排》示例

国际财务报告准则第 11 号——合营安排

目　　录

		段落
1	建造服务	2-8
2	共同经营的购物中心	9-13
3	产品的共同制造和配送	14-28
4	共同经营的银行	29-33
5	油气勘探、开采和生产活动	34-43
6	液化天然气安排	44-52

下列示例与《国际财务报告准则第 11 号》一并发布,但不构成其组成部分。它们举例说明了《国际财务报告准则第 11 号》的某些方面,但并非旨在提供解释性指南。

1. 下列示例以假定情况说明主体在不同情形下应用《国际财务报告准则第 11 号》可能运用的判断。尽管这些示例的有些方面可能按照实际情况呈现,但在应用《国际财务报告准则第 11 号》时,仍需要评价所有与特定的实际情况相关的事实和情形。

示例 1——建造服务

2. A 和 B(参与方)是两家公司,其业务是提供多种公共和私人建造服务。他们签署了一项合同安排,以共同完成一项与政府之间的合同,即设计并建造两个城市间一条道路。该合同安排确定了 A 和 B 公司的参与份额,明确了两方共同控制该安排,合同安排的主要事项是道路的移交。

3. 参与方成立了一个单独主体(主体 Z),通过主体 Z 实施该安排。主体 Z 代表 A 和 B 与政府签订合同。此外,有关该安排的资产和负债由主体 Z 持有。主体 Z 法律形式的主要特征是 A 和 B 参与方,而不是主体 Z,拥有这些资产,并承担其负债。

4. A 和 B 的合同安排还规定:

(1) A 和 B 根据其在该安排中的参与份额分享该安排相关活动所需的全部资产的权利;

(2) A 和 B 根据其在该安排中的参与份额分别或共同承担该安排相关活动的经营性和筹资性债务;

(3) A 和 B 根据其在该安排中的参与份额分享由该安排相关活动产生的损益。

5. 为了协调和监督这些活动,A 和 B 指定了一名将成为 A 或 B 雇员的经营者。在某一特定时间之后,该经营者的职责将轮转到另一参与方的雇员。A 和 B 同意由经营者所雇人员在"无利得或损失"的基础上进行这些活动。

6. 根据与政府签订的合同规定的条款,主体 Z 代表 A 和 B 向政府提供建造服务。

分析

7. 该合营安排通过单独主体执行,该单独主体的法律形式没有考虑参与方与单独主体之间的区分(即主体 Z 持有的资产和负债是 A 和 B 的资产和负债)。A 和 B 在合同安排中强调了这项规定,即该规定称 A 和 B 拥有与通过主体 Z 实施的该安排的资产,并承担其负债。该合营安排是共同经营。

8. A 和 B 根据其约定的参与份额在他们各自财务报表中确认这些资产(例如,不动产、厂场和设备以及应收账款)的份额,以及由该安排产生的负债(例如,对第三方的应付账款）的份额。A 和 B 也分别确认通过主体 Z 向政府提供建造服务产生的收入和费用的份额。

示例 2——共同经营的购物中心

9. 两家房地产公司（参与方）为并购和经营一家购物中心成立了一个单独主体（主体 X）。参与方的合同安排对主体 X 进行的活动设定了共同控制。主体 X 法律形式的主要特征是主体 X，而不是参与方，拥有与该安排相关的资产，并承担其负债。相关活动包括零售单元的出租、停车位的管理、购物中心及电梯等设备的维护、购物中心整体声誉和客户关系的建立。

10. 该合同安排的条款如下：

（1）主体 X 拥有该购物中心。该合同安排没有规定参与方有权拥有该购物中心。

（2）参与方不承担主体 X 的债务、负债或义务。如果主体 X 不能偿还其债务或其他负债，或者不能清偿第三方的义务，各参与方对第三方承担的负债仅限于该参与方出资额中未支付部分。

（3）参与方有权出售或抵押其在主体 X 中的权益。

（4）各参与方根据其在主体 X 中的权益分享购物中心经营收益（租金收益减经营成本后的净额）的份额。

分析

11. 合营安排通过一个单独主体执行，该主体的法律形式使其在自身立场上考虑问题（即该单独主体持有的资产和负债是其自身的资产和负债，不是参与方的资产和负债）。此外，合同安排的条款并未明确，参与方拥有与该安排相关的资产权利和负债义务。相反，合同安排的条款表明，参与方拥有主体 X 净资产的权利。

12. 根据上述规定，没有其他事实和情形表明参与方实质上拥有与该安排相关的资产的所有经济利益，并承担与该安排相关的负债义务。该合营安排是合营企业。

13. 参与方将其在主体 X 净资产中的权利确认为投资，使用权益法进行会计处理。

示例 3——产品的共同制造和配送

14. 企业 A 和 B（参与方）签订了一份战略性和经营性的安排（框架协议），在该协议中他们同意在不同市场共同生产和配送一项产品（产品 P）的条款。

15. 参与方同意通过签订合营安排进行生产和配送活动，这些活动如下：

（1）生产活动：参与方同意通过合营安排（即制造安排）进行生产活动。该制造安排通过一个单独主体（主体 M）进行构造，该工具的法律形式使其在自身立场上考虑问题（即主体 M 持有的资产和负债是其自身的资产和负债，不是参与方的资产和负债）。根据该框架协议，参与方承诺按照其在主体 M 中的所有者权益购买根据制造安排生产的所有产品 P。参与方随后向另一个由其共同控制的安排出售这些产品 P，并按照以下描述对产品 P 进行配送。处理 A 和 B 之间制造活动的框架协议和合同安排都没有表明参与方拥有与制造活动相关的资产权利和负债义务。

（2）配送活动：参与方同意通过合营安排（即配送安排）进行配送活动。该配送安排通过一个单独主体（主体 D）进行构造，该主体的法律形式使其在自身立场上考虑问题（即主体 D 持有的资产和负债是其自身的资产和负债，不是参与方的资产和负债）。根据该框架协议，配送安排按照不同市场需求从参与方订购产品 P，在这些市场上配送安排销售这些产品。处理 A 和 B 之间配送活动的框架协议和合同安排都没有表明参与方拥有与配送活动相关的资产权利和负债义务。

16. 此外，框架协议规定：

（1）制造安排将生产产品 P，以满足配送安排对参与方设定的产品 P 的需求；

（2）关于制造安排向参与方销售产品 P 的相关商业条款。制造安排将根据 A 和 B 同意的价格向参与方销售产品 P，以收回所有发生的生产成本。随后，参与方以 A 和 B 同意的价格向配送安排销售该产品。

（3）制造安排可能出现的任何现金短缺，都将由参与方根据其在主体 M 中的所有者权益进行出资。

分析

17. 框架协议设定了参与方 A 和 B 制造和配送产品 P 的条款。这些活动通过合营安排进行，旨在制造和配送产品 P。

18. 参与方通过主体 M 执行制造安排，主体 M 的法律形式区分了参与方和该主体。处理制造活动的框架协议和合同安排都没有表明参与方拥有与制造活动相关的资产权利和负债义务。然而，当考虑以下事实和情况时，参与方决定该制造安排是共同经营：

（1）参与方承诺购买根据制造安排生产的所有产品 P。因此，参与方实质上拥有与该安排相关的资产的所有经济利益。

（2）制造安排生产产品 P，以满足参与方的数量和质量要求，从而实现配送安排对产品 P 的需求。制造安排仅取决于参与方对现金流的产生及其承诺当制造安排发生任何现金短缺时提供资金，这表明参与方对制造安排的负债承担义务，因为这些负债将通过参与方购买产品 P 进行清偿或直接由参与方提供资金。

19. 参与方通过主体 D 进行配送活动，主体 D 的法律形式区分了参与方和该主体。此外，处理配送活动的框架协议和合同安排都没有表明参与方拥有与配送活动相关的资产权利和负债义务。

20. 没有其他事实和情形表明参与方实质上拥有与该安排相关的资产的所有经济利益，参与方承担与该安排相关的负债义务。该合营安排是合营企业。

21. A 和 B 根据其在主体 M 中的所有者权益，各自在财务报表中确认由制造安排产生的资产（例如，不动产、厂场和设备，现金）的份额和负债（例如，对第三方的应付账款）的份额。各参与方也确认由制造安排产生的生产产品 P 费用份额，以及销售产品 P 给配送安排相关的收入份额。

22. 参与方将其在配送安排中对净资产的权利确认为投资，并以权益法进行会计处理。

变动

23. 假定参与方同意上述制造安排不仅负责产品 P 的生产，还负责向第三方客户配送。

24. 参与方也同意建立与上述配送安排相似的专门配送产品 P 的配送安排，以帮助将产品 P 配送至其他特定市场。

25. 制造安排也直接向配送安排销售产品 P。配送安排没有承诺购买或保留固定比例的制造安排产量。

分析

26. 上述变动既不影响从事制造活动的单独主体的法律形式，也不影响参与方对制造活动相关的资产权利和负债义务的合同条款。然而，它使得制造安排成为一项自我融资的安排，因为它能出于自身利益的考虑与第三方客户进行交易并配送产品 P，因此，自己负责需求、存货和信用风险。尽管制造安排还可以向配送安排销售产品 P，在这种情况下，制造安排不依赖于那些能够在持续的基础上执行其活动的参与方。如果这样，该制造安排就是合营企业。

27. 上述变动没有影响到该配送安排分类为合营企业。

28. 参与方将其在制造安排中对净资产的权利和在配送安排中对净资产的权利确认为投资，并以权益法进行会计处理。

示例 4——共同经营的银行

29. 银行 A 和 B（参与方）同意通过建立一个单独主体（银行 C）合并他们的经营、投资银行、资产管理和服务活动。双方预期该安排能从几个方面使他们受益。银行 A 认为，该安排能使其通过扩大产品和服务的提供而获得发掘潜能高速增长的机会，实现扩大规模的战略计划。银行 B 预期该安排能增强其金融储蓄和市场产品的提供能力。

30. 银行 C 法律形式的主要特征是，使其在自身立场上考虑问题（即该单独主体持有的资产和负债是其自身的资产和负债，不是参与方的资产和负债）。银行 A 和 B 各自持有银行 C 的 40% 所有者权益，剩余 20% 公开发行并被广泛持有。银行 A 和 B 的股东同意共同控制银行 C 的经营活动。

31. 此外，银行 A 和 B 签订了不可撤销协议，即使双方争执，如果需要的话，两家银行同意共同或各自提供相同数量的必要资金，以确保银行 C 符合适用的法律和银行监管要求，并履行其向银行监管部门所作的承诺。该承诺代表各方支付所需资金的 50%，以确保银行 C 符合法律和银行的监管要求。

分析

32. 该合营安排通过一个单独主体被执行，该工具的法律形式区分了参与方和该单独主体。合同的条款没有明确参与方拥有银行 C 的资产权利和负债义务，但它规定参与方对银行 C 的净资产拥有权利。当银行 C 不能够符合适用的法律和银行监管要求时，参与方向银行 C 提供支持的承诺并不是参与方对银行 C 的负债承担义务的决定因素。没有其他事实和情形表明参与方实质上拥有与银行 C 相关的资产的所有经济利益并承担与银行 C 相关的负债义务。该合营安排是合营企业。

33. 银行 A 和 B 都将其在银行 C 中对净资产的权利确认为投资，并以权益法进行会计处理。

示例 5——油气勘探、开采和生产活动

34. 公司 A 和 B（参与方）成立了一个单独主体（主体 H）和一项共同经营安排，在国家 O 进行油气勘探、开采和生产活动。主体 H 法律形式的主要特征是，使其在自身立场上考虑问题（即该单独主体持有的资产和负债是其自身的资产和负债，不是参与方的资产和负债）。

35. 国家 O 授权主体 H 在特定区域（油田）进行油气勘探、开采和生产活动。

36. 股东之间的协议和参与方同意的共同经营安排明确了他们在这些活动中的权利和义务。这些协议的主要条款总结如下：

股东之间的协议

37. 主体 H 的董事会由各参与方的一名董事组成。各参与方拥有主体 H 50% 的所有者权益。通过任何决议需要所有董事的一致同意。

共同经营安排

38. 共同经营安排成立了一个运营委员会。该委员会由各参与方的一名代表组成。各参与方拥有运营委员会50%的参与权益。

39. 运营委员会批准相关活动的预算和工作计划，这也需要各参与方代表的一致同意。其中一方被任命为经营者，负责管理和执行批准的工作计划。

40. 共同经营安排明确，勘探、开采和生产活动产生的权利和义务应根据参与方在主体H中所有者权益的比例进行分摊。尤其是，共同经营安排规定，参与方分享：

（1）主体H取得的勘探、开采许可产生的权利和义务（例如，许可、复原负债、矿区土地使用费和应交所得税）；

（2）获得的产品；以及

（3）与所有工作计划相关的所有成本。

41. 与所有工作计划相关的成本可由各参与方的现金求偿权补偿。如果任何一方不能偿还其货币性义务，另一方被要求向主体H提供违约的金额。违约金额作为违约方欠另一方的债务。

分析

42. 参与方通过合营安排执行一个单独主体，该工具的法律形式区分了参与方和该单独主体。参与方能够取消对由该单独主体的法律形式产生的权利和义务的评价，其中该安排是通过这个单独主体执行的。他们已经通过共同经营安排的条款这么作了，该共同经营安排使参与方拥有主体H的资产权利（例如，勘探和开采的许可、生产以及由这些活动产生的其他资产）和负债义务（例如，由工作计划产生的所有成本和义务）。该合营安排是共同经营。

43. 公司A和B根据其同意的参与份额在他们各自财务报表中确认这些资产的份额，以及由该安排产生的负债的份额。在此基础上，各方也分别确认（从销售生产份额中获得的）收入和费用的份额。

示例6——液化天然气安排

44. 公司A拥有一个蕴含大量天然气资源的未开采气田。公司A决定，只有在这些气体出售给海外市场的客户时，该气田才能实现其经济利益。为此，需要建设一套液化天然气设备，液化这些气体，以便用船运送到海外市场。

45. 为开采并经营气田和液化天然气设备，公司A和公司B签订一项合营安排。在该安排下，公司A和B（参与方）同意各自分别以气田和现金向一个新成立的单独主体（主体C）出资。参与方各获得主体C 50%的所有者权益，作为其出资的回报。主体C法律形式的主要特征是，使其在自身立场上考虑问题（即该单独主体持有的资产和负债是其自身的资产和负债，不是参与方的资产和负债）。

46. 参与方之间的合同安排规定：

（1）公司A和B必须各自在主体C的董事会中任命两位成员。主体C作出的战略和投资，必须得到董事会的一致同意。

（2）气田和液化天然气设备的日常管理，包括开采和建设活动，应由公司B的职员根据参与方一致同意的决定具体负责。主体C将偿付公司B在管理气田和液化天然气设备过程中发生的成本。

（3）主体C负责承担生产和销售液化天然气过程中的所得税、矿区土地使用费，以及日常经营过程中的其他负债，比如，应付账款、场地复原和退役负债。

（4）公司A和B对由该安排中进行的活动所产生的利润拥有相同份额，因此，他们对主体C发放的股利也拥有相同份额。

47. 合同安排没有规定任何一方拥有主体C的资产权利和负债义务。

48. 主体C的董事会决定与债权人财团签订一份融资安排，为气田的开采和液化天然气设备的建设筹集资金。开采和建设的预计总成本为1000百万货币单位。

49. 该财团向主体C提供了700货币单位百万的贷款。该安排规定，只有当主体C在开采气田和建设液化天然气设备过程中违约时，该财团对公司A和B才有追索权。该财团同意，一旦液化天然气设备开始建设，该财团对公司A和B就没有追索权，因为经评估，主体C从液化天然气的销售获得的现金流足以偿还贷款。尽管在此时该财团对公司A和B没有追索权，但该财团还是通过持有液化天然气设备的留置权作为主体C违约的担保。

分析

50. 该合营安排通过一个单独主体被执行，该工具的法律形式区分了参与方和该独立工具。合同安排的条款没有明确参与方拥有主体C的资产权利和负债义务，但它规定参与方对主体C的净资产拥有权利。在气田开采和液化天然气设备建设过程中的筹融资协议的资源性质（即公司A和B在这一阶段分别提供了担保）本身也没有使参与方承担主体C负债（即贷款是主体C的一项负债）的义务。公司A和B有独立的负债，该负债是当主体C无法偿还开采和建设过程中的贷款时偿还该贷款的担保。

51. 没有其他事实和情形表明参与方实质上拥有与主体C相关的资产的所有经济利益并承担与主体C相关的负债义务。该合营安排是合营企业。

52. 公司A和B都将其在主体C中对净资产的权利确认为投资，并以权益法进行会计处理。

IFRS 11 JOINT ARRANGEMENTS

International Financial Reporting Standard 11
Joint Arrangements

IFRS 11 JOINT ARRANGEMENTS

CONTENTS

INTRODUCTION	INI – INI 1
INTERNATIONAL FINANCIAL REPORTING STANDARD 11 *JOINT ARRANGEMENTS*	
OBJECTIVE	1 – 2
SCOPE	3
JOINT ARRANGEMENTS	4 – 19
Joint control	7 – 13
Types of joint arrangement	14 – 19
FINANCIAL STATEMENTS OF PARTIES TO A JOINT ARRANGEMENT	20 – 25
Joint operation	20 – 23
Joint venture	24 – 25
SEPARATE FINANCIAL STATEMENTS	26 – 27

APPENDICES

A Defined terms

B Application guidance

C Effective date, transition and withdrawal of other IFRSs

APPROVAL BY THE BOARD OF IFRS 11 ISSUED IN MAY 2011

IFRS 11 JOINT ARRANGEMENTS

International Financial Reporting Standard 11 *Joint Arrangements* (IFRS 11) is set out in paragraphs 1–27 and Appendices A–D. All the paragraphs have equal authority. Paragraphs in **bold type** state the main principles. Terms defined in Appendix A are in italics the first time they appear in the Standard. Definitions of other terms are given in the Glossary for International Financial Reporting Standards. IFRS 11 should be read in the context of its objective and the Basis for Conclusions, the *Preface to International Financial Reporting Standards and the Conceptual Framework for Financial Reporting*. IAS 8 *Accounting Policies, Changes in Accounting Estimates and Errors* provides a basis for selecting and applying accounting policies in the absence of explicit guidance.

IFRS 11 JOINT ARRANGEMENTS

Introduction

Overview

IN1 International Financial Reporting Standard 11 *Joint Arrangements* establishes principles for financial reporting by parties to a joint arrangement.

IN2 The IFRS supersedes IAS 31 *Interests in Joint Ventures* and SIC – 13 *Jointly Controlled Entities-Non-Monetary Contributions by Venturers* and is effective for annual periods beginning on or after 1 January 2013. Earlier application is permitted.

Reasons for issuing the IFRS

IN3 The IFRS is concerned principally with addressing two aspects of IAS 31: first, that the structure of the arrangement was the only determinant of the accounting and, second, that an entity had a choice of accounting treatment for interests in jointly controlled entities.

IN4 IFRS 11 improves on IAS 31 by establishing principles that are applicable to the accounting for all joint arrangements.

Main features of the IFRS

IN5 The IFRS requires a party to a joint arrangement to determine the type of joint arrangement in which it is involved by assessing its rights and obligations arising from the arrangement.

General requirements

IN6 The IFRS is to be applied by all entities that are a party to a joint arrangement. A joint arrangement is an arrangement of which two or more parties have joint control. The IFRS defines joint control as the contractually agreed sharing of control of an arrangement, which exists only when decisions about the relevant activities (ie activities that significantly affect the returns of the arrangement) require the unanimous consent of the parties sharing control.

IN7 The IFRS classifies joint arrangements into two types-joint operations and joint ventures. A joint operation is a joint arrangement whereby the parties that have joint control of the arrangement (ie joint operators) have rights to the assets, and obligations for the liabilities, relating to the arrangement. A joint venture is a joint arrangement whereby

IFRS 11 JOINT ARRANGEMENTS

the parties that have joint control of the arrangement (ie joint venturers) have rights to the net assets of the arrangement.

IN8 An entity determines the type of joint arrangement in which it is involved by considering its rights and obligations. An entity assesses its rights and obligations by considering the structure and legal form of the arrangement, the contractual terms agreed to by the parties to the arrangement and, when relevant, other facts and circumstances.

IN9 The IFRS requires a joint operator to recognise and measure the assets and liabilities (and recognise the related revenues and expenses) in relation to its interest in the arrangement in accordance with relevant IFRSs applicable to the particular assets, liabilities, revenues and expenses.

IN10 The IFRS requires a joint venturer to recognise an investment and to account for that investment using the equity method in accordance with IAS 28 *Investments in Associates and Joint Ventures*, unless the entity is exempted from applying the equity method as specified in that standard.

IN11 The disclosure requirements for parties with joint control of a joint arrangement are specified in IFRS 12 *Disclosure of Interests in Other Entities*.

International Financial Reporting Standard 11
Joint Arrangements

Objective

1   The objective of this IFRS is to establish principles for financial reporting by entities that have an interest in arrangements that are controlled jointly (ie *joint arrangements*).

Meeting the objective

2   To meet the objective in paragraph 1, this IFRS defines *joint control* and requires an entity that is a *party to a joint arrangement* to determine the type of joint arrangement in which it is involved by assessing its rights and obligations and to account for those rights and obligations in accordance with that type of joint arrangement.

Scope

3   **This IFRS shall be applied by all entities that are a party to a joint arrangement.**

Joint arrangements

4   **A joint arrangement is an arrangement of which two or more parties have joint control.**

5   **A joint arrangement has the following characteristics:**

   (a)   **The parties are bound by a contractual arrangement (see paragraphs B2 – B4).**

   (b)   **The contractual arrangement gives two or more of those parties joint control of the arrangement (see paragraphs 7 – 13).**

6   **A joint arrangement is either a *joint operation* or a *joint venture*.**

Joint control

7   **Joint control is the contractually agreed sharing of control of an arrangement, which exists only when decisions about the relevant activities require the unanimous consent of the parties sharing control.**

8   An entity that is a party to an arrangement shall assess whether the contractual arrangement gives all the parties, or a group of the parties, control of the arrangement

collectively. All the parties, or a group of the parties, control the arrangement collectively when they must act together to direct the activities that significantly affect the returns of the arrangement (ie the relevant activities).

9 Once it has been determined that all the parties, or a group of the parties, control the arrangement collectively, joint control exists only when decisions about the relevant activities require the unanimous consent of the parties that control the arrangement collectively.

10 In a joint arrangement, no single party controls the arrangement on its own. A party with joint control of an arrangement can prevent any of the other parties, or a group of the parties, from controlling the arrangement.

11 An arrangement can be a joint arrangement even though not all of its parties have joint control of the arrangement. This IFRS distinguishes between parties that have joint control of a joint arrangement (*joint operators* or *joint venturers*) and parties that participate in, but do not have joint control of, a joint arrangement.

12 An entity will need to apply judgement when assessing whether all the parties, or a group of the parties, have joint control of an arrangement. An entity shall make this assessment by considering all facts and circumstances (see paragraphs B5 – B11).

13 If facts and circumstances change, an entity shall reassess whether it still has joint control of the arrangement.

Types of joint arrangement

14 **An entity shall determine the type of joint arrangement in which it is involved. The classification of a joint arrangement as a joint operation or a joint venture depends upon the rights and obligations of the parties to the arrangement.**

15 **A joint operation is a joint arrangement whereby the parties that have joint control of the arrangement have rights to the assets, and obligations for the liabilities, relating to the arrangement. Those parties are called joint operators.**

16 **A joint venture is a joint arrangement whereby the parties that have joint control of the arrangement have rights to the net assets of the arrangement. Those parties are called joint venturers.**

17 An entity applies judgement when assessing whether a joint arrangement is a joint operation or a joint venture. An entity shall determine the type of joint arrangement in which it is involved by considering its rights and obligations arising from the

18 arrangement. An entity assesses its rights and obligations by considering the structure and legal form of the arrangement, the terms agreed by the parties in the contractual arrangement and, when relevant, other facts and circumstances (see paragraphs B12 – B33).

18 Sometimes the parties are bound by a framework agreement that sets up the general contractual terms for undertaking one or more activities. The framework agreement might set out that the parties establish different joint arrangements to deal with specific activities that form part of the agreement. Even though those joint arrangements are related to the same framework agreement, their type might be different if the parties' rights and obligations differ when undertaking the different activities dealt with in the framework agreement. Consequently, joint operations and joint ventures can coexist when the parties undertake different activities that form part of the same framework agreement.

19 If facts and circumstances change, an entity shall reassess whether the type of joint arrangement in which it is involved has changed.

Financial statements of parties to a joint arrangement

Joint operations

20 **A joint operator shall recognise in relation to its interest in a joint operation:**

(a) **its assets, including its share of any assets held jointly;**

(b) **its liabilities, including its share of any liabilities incurred jointly;**

(c) **its revenue from the sale of its share of the output arising from the joint operation;**

(d) **its share of the revenue from the sale of the output by the joint operation; and**

(e) **its expenses, including its share of any expenses incurred jointly.**

21 A joint operator shall account for the assets, liabilities, revenues and expenses relating to its interest in a joint operation in accordance with the IFRSs applicable to the particular assets, liabilities, revenues and expenses.

22 The accounting for transactions such as the sale, contribution or purchase of assets between an entity and a joint operation in which it is a joint operator is specified in paragraphs B34 – B37.

23 A party that participates in, but does not have joint control of, a joint operation shall also account for its interest in the arrangement in accordance with paragraphs 20 – 22 if that party has rights to the assets, and obligations for the liabilities, relating to the joint operation. If a party that participates in, but does not have joint control of, a joint operation does not have rights to the assets, and obligations for the liabilities, relating to that joint operation, it shall account for its interest in the joint operation in accordance with the IFRSs applicable to that interest.

Joint ventures

24 **A joint venturer shall recognise its interest in a joint venture as an investment and shall account for that investment using the equity method in accordance with IAS 28** *Investments in Associates and Joint Ventures* **unless the entity is exempted from applying the equity method as specified in that standard.**

25 A party that participates in, but does not have joint control of, a joint venture shall account for its interest in the arrangement in accordance with IFRS 9 *Financial Instruments*, unless it has significant influence over the joint venture, in which case it shall account for it in accordance with IAS 28 (as amended in 2011).

Separate financial statements

26 **In its separate financial statements, a joint operator or joint venturer shall account for its interest in:**

   (a) a joint operation in accordance with paragraphs 20 – 22;

   (b) a joint venture in accordance with paragraph 10 of IAS 27 *Separate Financial Statements.*

27 **In its separate financial statements, a party that participates in, but does not have joint control of, a joint arrangement shall account for its interest in:**

   (a) a joint operation in accordance with paragraph 23;

   (b) a joint venture in accordance with IFRS 9, unless the entity has significant influence over the joint venture, in which case it shall apply paragraph 10 of IAS 27 (as amended in 2011).

Appendix A
Defined terms

This appendix is an integral part of the IFRS.

joint arrangement	An arrangement of which two or more parties have **joint control**.
joint control	The contractually agreed sharing of control of an arrangement, which exists only when decisions about the relevant activities require the unanimous consent of the parties sharing control.
joint operation	A **joint arrangement** whereby the parties that have **joint control** of the arrangement have rights to the assets, and obligations for the liabilities, relating to the arrangement.
joint operator	A party to a **joint operation** that has **joint control** of that joint operation.
joint venture	A j**oint arrangement** whereby the parties that have **joint control** of the arrangement have rights to the net assets of the arrangement.
joint venturer	A party to a **joint venture** that has **joint control** of that joint venture.
party to a joint arrangement	An entity that participates in a **joint arrangement**, regardless of whether that entity has **joint control** of the arrangement.
separate vehicle	A separately identifiable financial structure, including separate legal entities or entities recognised by statute, regardless of whether those entities have a legal personality.

IFRS 11 JOINT ARRANGEMENTS

The following terms are defined in IAS 27 (as amended in 2011), IAS 28 (as amended in 2011) or IFRS 10 *Consolidated Financial Statements* and are used in this IFRS with the meanings specified in those IFRSs:

- control of an investee
- equity method
- power
- protective rights
- relevant activities
- separate financial statements
- significant influence.

Appendix B
Application guidance

This appendix is an integral part of the IFRS. It describes the application of paragraphs 1 – 27 and has the same authority as the other parts of the IFRS.

B1 The examples in this appendix portray hypothetical situations. Although some aspects of the examples may be present in actual fact patterns, all relevant facts and circumstances of a particular fact pattern would need to be evaluated when applying IFRS 11.

Joint arrangements

Contractual arrangement (paragraph 5)

B2 Contractual arrangements can be evidenced in several ways. An enforceable contractual arrangement is often, but not always, in writing, usually in the form of a contract or documented discussions between the parties. Statutory mechanisms can also create enforceable arrangements, either on their own or in conjunction with contracts between the parties.

B3 When joint arrangements are structured through a *separate vehicle* (see paragraphs B19 – B33), the contractual arrangement, or some aspects of the contractual arrangement, will in some cases be incorporated in the articles, charter or by-laws of the separate vehicle.

B4 The contractual arrangement sets out the terms upon which the parties participate in the activity that is the subject of the arrangement. The contractual arrangement generally deals with such matters as:

(a) the purpose, activity and duration of the joint arrangement.

(b) how the members of the board of directors, or equivalent governing body, of the joint arrangement, are appointed.

(c) the decision-making process: the matters requiring decisions from the parties, the voting rights of the parties and the required level of support for those matters. The decision-making process reflected in the contractual arrangement establishes joint control of the arrangement (see paragraphs B5 – B11).

(d) the capital or other contributions required of the parties.

(e) how the parties share assets, liabilities, revenues, expenses or profit or loss relating to the joint arrangement.

Joint control (paragraphs 7 - 13)

B5 In assessing whether an entity has joint control of an arrangement, an entity shall assess first whether all the parties, or a group of the parties, control the arrangement. IFRS 10 defines control and shall be used to determine whether all the parties, or a group of the parties, are exposed, or have rights, to variable returns from their involvement with the arrangement and have the ability to affect those returns through their power over the arrangement. When all the parties, or a group of the parties, considered collectively, are able to direct the activities that significantly affect the returns of the arrangement (ie the relevant activities), the parties control the arrangement collectively.

B6 After concluding that all the parties, or a group of the parties, control the arrangement collectively, an entity shall assess whether it has joint control of the arrangement. Joint control exists only when decisions about the relevant activities require the unanimous consent of the parties that collectively control the arrangement. Assessing whether the arrangement is jointly controlled by all of its parties or by a group of the parties, or controlled by one of its parties alone, can require judgement.

B7 Sometimes the decision-making process that is agreed upon by the parties in their contractual arrangement implicitly leads to joint control. For example, assume two parties establish an arrangement in which each has 50 per cent of the voting rights and the contractual arrangement between them specifies that at least 51 per cent of the voting rights are required to make decisions about the relevant activities. In this case, the parties have implicitly agreed that they have joint control of the arrangement because decisions about the relevant activities cannot be made without both parties agreeing.

B8 In other circumstances, the contractual arrangement requires a minimum proportion of the voting rights to make decisions about the relevant activities. When that minimum required proportion of the voting rights can be achieved by more than one combination of the parties agreeing together, that arrangement is not a joint arrangement unless the contractual arrangement specifies which parties (or combination of parties) are required to agree unanimously to decisions about the relevant activities of the arrangement.

> **Application examples**
>
> **Example 1**
>
> Assume that three parties establish an arrangement: A has 50 per cent of the voting rights in the arrangement, B has 30 per cent and C has 20 per cent. The contractual arrangement between A, B and C specifies that at least 75 per cent of the voting rights are required to make decisions about the relevant activities of the arrangement. Even though A can block any decision, it does not control the arrangement because it needs the agreement of B. The terms of their contractual arrangement requiring at least 75 per cent of the voting rights to make decisions about the relevant activities imply that A and B have joint control of the arrangement because decisions about the relevant activities of the arrangement cannot be made without both A and B agreeing.
>
> **Example 2**
>
> Assume an arrangement has three parties: A has 50 per cent of the voting rights in the arrangement and B and C each have 25 per cent. The contractual arrangement between A, B and C specifies that at least 75 per cent of the voting rights are required to make decisions about the relevant activities of the arrangement. Even though A can block any decision, it does not control the arrangement because it needs the agreement of either B or C. In this example, A, B and C collectively control the arrangement. However, there is more than one combination of parties that can agree to reach 75 per cent of the voting rights (ie either A and B or A and C). In such a situation, to be a joint arrangement the contractual arrangement between the parties would need to specify which combination of the parties is required to agree unanimously to decisions about the relevant activities of the arrangement.
>
> **Example 3**
>
> Assume an arrangement in which A and B each have 35 per cent of the voting rights in the arrangement with the remaining 30 per cent being widely dispersed. Decisions about the relevant activities require approval by a majority of the voting rights. A and B have joint control of the arrangement only if the contractual arrangement specifies that decisions about the relevant activities of the arrangement require both A and B agreeing.

B9 The requirement for unanimous consent means that any party with joint control of the arrangement can prevent any of the other parties, or a group of the parties, from making unilateral decisions (about the relevant activities) without its consent. If the requirement for unanimous consent relates only to decisions that give a party protective rights and not to decisions about the relevant activities of an arrangement, that party is not a party with joint control of the arrangement.

B10   A contractual arrangement might include clauses on the resolution of disputes, such as arbitration. These provisions may allow for decisions to be made in the absence of unanimous consent among the parties that have joint control. The existence of such provisions does not prevent the arrangement from being jointly controlled and, consequently, from being a joint arrangement.

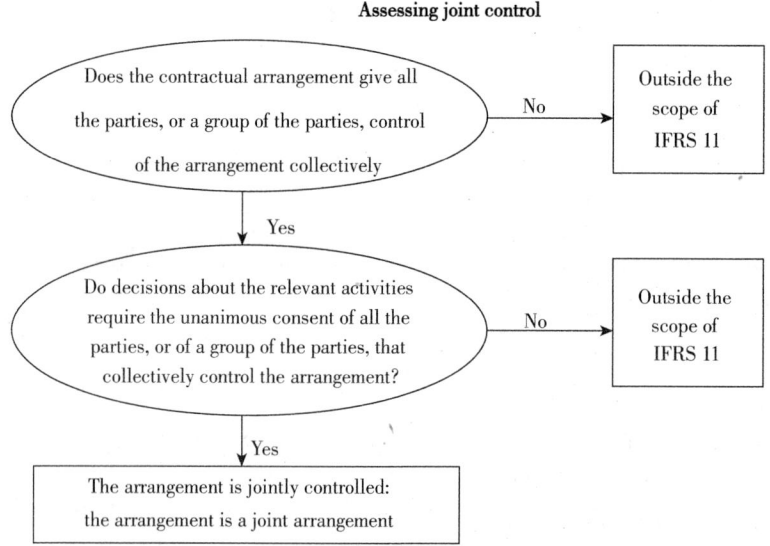

B11   When an arrangement is outside the scope of IFRS 11, an entity accounts for its interest in the arrangement in accordance with relevant IFRSs, such as IFRS 10, IAS 28 (as amended in 2011) or IFRS 9.

Types of joint arrangement (paragraphs 14 - 19)

B12   Joint arrangements are established for a variety of purposes (eg as a way for parties to share costs and risks, or as a way to provide the parties with access to new technology or new markets), and can be established using different structures and legal forms.

B13   Some arrangements do not require the activity that is the subject of the arrangement to be undertaken in a separate vehicle. However, other arrangements involve the establishment of a separate vehicle.

B14　The classification of joint arrangements required by this IFRS depends upon the parties' rights and obligations arising from the arrangement in the normal course of business. This IFRS classifies joint arrangements as either joint operations or joint ventures. When an entity has rights to the assets, and obligations for the liabilities, relating to the arrangement, the arrangement is a joint operation. When an entity has rights to the net assets of the arrangement, the arrangement is a joint venture. Paragraphs B16 – B33 set out the assessment an entity carries out to determine whether it has an interest in a joint operation or an interest in a joint venture.

Classification of a joint arrangement

B15　As stated in paragraph B14, the classification of joint arrangements requires the parties to assess their rights and obligations arising from the arrangement. When making that assessment, an entity shall consider the following:

(a)　the structure of the joint arrangement (see paragraphs B16 – B21).

(b)　when the joint arrangement is structured through a separate vehicle:

(ⅰ)　the legal form of the separate vehicle (see paragraphs B22 – B24);

(ⅱ)　the terms of the contractual arrangement (see paragraphs B25 – B28); and

(ⅲ)　when relevant, other facts and circumstances (see paragraphs B29 – B33).

Structure of the joint arrangement

Joint arrangements not structured through a separate vehicle

B16　A joint arrangement that is not structured through a separate vehicle is a joint operation. In such cases, the contractual arrangement establishes the parties' rights to the assets, and obligations for the liabilities, relating to the arrangement, and the parties' rights to the corresponding revenues and obligations for the corresponding expenses.

B17　The contractual arrangement often describes the nature of the activities that are the subject of the arrangement and how the parties intend to undertake those activities together. For example, the parties to a joint arrangement could agree to manufacture a product together, with each party being responsible for a specific task and each using its own assets and incurring its own liabilities. The contractual arrangement could also specify how the revenues and expenses that are common to the parties are to be shared among them. In such a case, each joint operator recognises in its financial statements the assets and liabilities used for the specific task, and recognises its share of the revenues and expenses in accordance with the contractual arrangement.

B18 In other cases, the parties to a joint arrangement might agree, for example, to share and operate an asset together. In such a case, the contractual arrangement establishes the parties' rights to the asset that is operated jointly, and how output or revenue from the asset and operating costs are shared among the parties. Each joint operator accounts for its share of the joint asset and its agreed share of any liabilities, and recognises its share of the output, revenues and expenses in accordance with the contractual arrangement.

Joint arrangements structured through a separate vehicle

B19 A joint arrangement in which the assets and liabilities relating to the arrangement are held in a separate vehicle can be either a joint venture or a joint operation.

B20 Whether a party is a joint operator or a joint venturer depends on the party's rights to the assets, and obligations for the liabilities, relating to the arrangement that are held in the separate vehicle.

B21 As stated in paragraph B15, when the parties have structured a joint arrangement in a separate vehicle, the parties need to assess whether the legal form of the separate vehicle, the terms of the contractual arrangement and, when relevant, any other facts and circumstances give them:

(a) rights to the assets, and obligations for the liabilities, relating to the arrangement (ie the arrangement is a joint operation); or

(b) rights to the net assets of the arrangement (ie the arrangement is a joint venture).

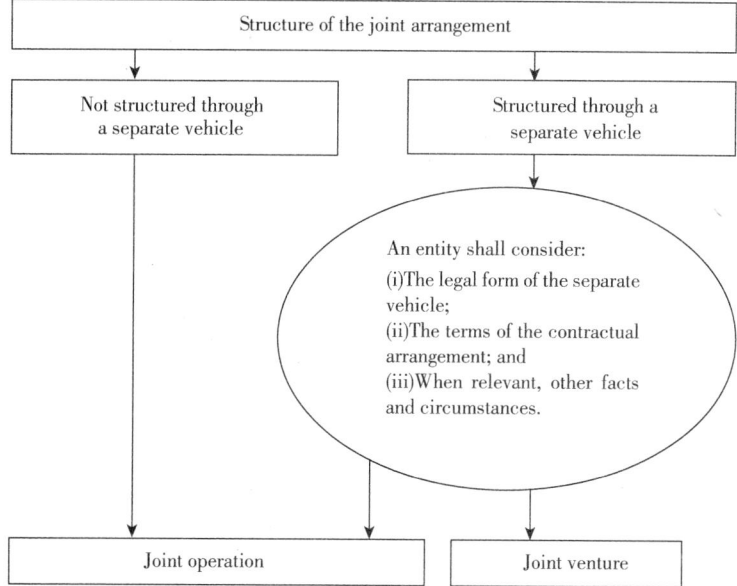

The legal form of the separate vehicle

B22 The legal form of the separate vehicle is relevant when assessing the type of joint arrangement. The legal form assists in the initial assessment of the parties' rights to the assets and obligations for the liabilities held in the separate vehicle, such as whether the parties have interests in the assets held in the separate vehicle and whether they are liable for the liabilities held in the separate vehicle.

B23 For example, the parties might conduct the joint arrangement through a separate vehicle, whose legal form causes the separate vehicle to be considered in its own right (ie the assets and liabilities held in the separate vehicle are the assets and liabilities of the separate vehicle and not the assets and liabilities of the parties). In such a case, the assessment of the rights and obligations conferred upon the parties by the legal form of the separate vehicle indicates that the arrangement is a joint venture. However, the terms agreed by the parties in their contractual arrangement (see paragraphs B25 – B28) and, when relevant, other facts and circumstances (see paragraphs B29 – B33) can override the assessment of the rights and obligations conferred upon the parties by the legal form of the separate vehicle.

B24　　The assessment of the rights and obligations conferred upon the parties by the legal form of the separate vehicle is sufficient to conclude that the arrangement is a joint operation only if the parties conduct the joint arrangement in a separate vehicle whose legal form does not confer separation between the parties and the separate vehicle (ie the assets and liabilities held in the separate vehicle are the parties' assets and liabilities).

Assessing the terms of the contractual arrangement

B25　　In many cases, the rights and obligations agreed to by the parties in their contractual arrangements are consistent, or do not conflict, with the rights and obligations conferred on the parties by the legal form of the separate vehicle in which the arrangement has been structured.

B26　　In other cases, the parties use the contractual arrangement to reverse or modify the rights and obligations conferred by the legal form of the separate vehicle in which the arrangement has been structured.

Application example

Example 4

Assume that two parties structure a joint arrangement in an incorporated entity. Each party has a 50 per cent ownership interest in the incorporated entity. The incorporation enables the separation of the entity from its owners and as a consequence the assets and liabilities held in the entity are the assets and liabilities of the incorporated entity. In such a case, the assessment of the rights and obligations conferred upon the parties by the legal form of the separate vehicle indicates that the parties have rights to the net assets of the arrangement.

However, the parties modify the features of the corporation through their contractual arrangement so that each has an interest in the assets of the incorporated entity and each is liable for the liabilities of the incorporated entity in a specified proportion. Such contractual modifications to the features of a corporation can cause an arrangement to be a joint operation.

B27　　The following table compares common terms in contractual arrangements of parties to a joint operation and common terms in contractual arrangements of parties to a joint venture. The examples of the contractual terms provided in the following table are not exhaustive.

IFRS 11 JOINT ARRANGEMENTS

Assessing the terms of the contractual arrangement		
	Joint operation	Joint venture
The terms of the contractual arrangement	The contractual arrangement provides the parties to the joint arrangement with rights to the assets, and obligations for the liabilities, relating to the arrangement.	The contractual arrangement provides the parties to the joint arrangement with rights to the net assets of the arrangement (ie it is the separate vehicle, not the parties, that has rights to the assets, and obligations for the liabilities, relating to the arrangement).
Rights to assets	The contractual arrangement establishes that the parties to the joint arrangement share all interests (eg rights, title or ownership) in the assets relating to the arrangement in a specified proportion (eg in proportion to the parties' ownership interest in the arrangement or in proportion to the activity carried out through the arrangement that is directly attributed to them).	The contractual arrangement establishes that the assets brought into the arrangement or subsequently acquired by the joint arrangement are the arrangement's assets. The parties have no interests (ie no rights, title or ownership) in the assets of the arrangement.
Obligations for liabilities	The contractual arrangement establishes that the parties to the joint arrangement share all liabilities, obligations, costs and expenses in a specified proportion (eg in proportion to the parties' ownership interest in the arrangement or in proportion to the activity carried out through the arrangement that is directly attributed to them).	The contractual arrangement establishes that the joint arrangement is liable for the debts and obligations of the arrangement.
		The contractual arrangement establishes that the parties to the joint arrangement are liable to the arrangement only to the extent of their respective investments in the arrangement or to their respective obligations to contribute any unpaid or additional capital to the arrangement, or both.
	The contractual arrangement establishes that the parties to the joint arrangement are liable for claims raised by third parties.	The contractual arrangement states that creditors of the joint arrangement do not have rights of recourse against any party with respect to debts or obligations of the arrangement.

Assessing the terms of the contractual arrangement		
	Joint operation	Joint venture
Revenues, expenses, profit or loss	The contractual arrangement establishes the allocation of revenues and expenses on the basis of the relative performance of each party to the joint arrangement. For example, the contractual arrangement might establish that revenues and expenses are allocated on the basis of the capacity that each party uses in a plant operated jointly, which could differ from their ownership interest in the joint arrangement. In other instances, the parties might have agreed to share the profit or loss relating to the arrangement on the basis of a specified proportion such as the parties' ownership interest in the arrangement. This would not prevent the arrangement from being a joint operation if the parties have rights to the assets, and obligations for the liabilities, relating to the arrangement.	The contractual arrangement establishes each party's share in the profit or loss relating to the activities of the arrangement.
Guarantees	The parties to joint arrangements are often required to provide guarantees to third parties that, for example, receive a service from, or provide financing to, the joint arrangement. The provision of such guarantees, or the commitment by the parties to provide them, does not, by itself, determine that the joint arrangement is a joint operation. The feature that determines whether the joint arrangement is a joint operation or a joint venture is whether the parties have obligations for the liabilities relating to the arrangement (for some of which the parties might or might not have provided a guarantee).	

B28 When the contractual arrangement specifies that the parties have rights to the assets, and obligations for the liabilities, relating to the arrangement, they are parties to a joint operation and do not need to consider other facts and circumstances (paragraphs B29 – B33) for the purposes of classifying the joint arrangement.

Assessing other facts and circumstances

B29   When the terms of the contractual arrangement do not specify that the parties have rights to the assets, and obligations for the liabilities, relating to the arrangement, the parties shall consider other facts and circumstances to assess whether the arrangement is a joint operation or a joint venture.

B30   A joint arrangement might be structured in a separate vehicle whose legal form confers separation between the parties and the separate vehicle. The contractual terms agreed among the parties might not specify the parties' rights to the assets and obligations for the liabilities, yet consideration of other facts and circumstances can lead to such an arrangement being classified as a joint operation. This will be the case when other facts and circumstances give the parties rights to the assets, and obligations for the liabilities, relating to the arrangement.

B31   When the activities of an arrangement are primarily designed for the provision of output to the parties, this indicates that the parties have rights to substantially all the economic benefits of the assets of the arrangement. The parties to such arrangements often ensure their access to the outputs provided by the arrangement by preventing the arrangement from selling output to third parties.

B32   The effect of an arrangement with such a design and purpose is that the liabilities incurred by the arrangement are, in substance, satisfied by the cash flows received from the parties through their purchases of the output. When the parties are substantially the only source of cash flows contributing to the continuity of the operations of the arrangement, this indicates that the parties have an obligation for the liabilities relating to the arrangement.

Application example

Example 5

Assume that two parties structure a joint arrangement in an incorporated entity (entity C) in which each party has a 50 per cent ownership interest. The purpose of the arrangement is to manufacture materials required by the parties for their own, individual manufacturing processes. The arrangement ensures that the parties operate the facility that produces the materials to the quantity and quality specifications of the parties.

The legal form of entity C (an incorporated entity) through which the activities are conducted initially indicates that the assets and liabilities held in entity C are the assets and liabilities of entity C. The contractual arrangement between the parties does not specify that the parties have rights to the assets or obligations for the liabilities of entity C. Accordingly, the legal form of entity C and the terms of the contractual arrangement indicate that the arrangement is a joint venture.

However, the parties also consider the following aspects of the arrangement:

- The parties agreed to purchase all the output produced by entity C in a ratio of 50:50. Entity C cannot sell any of the output to third parties, unless this is approved by the two parties to the arrangement. Because the purpose of the arrangement is to provide the parties with output they require, such sales to third parties are expected to be uncommon and not material.

- The price of the output sold to the parties is set by both parties at a level that is designed to cover the costs of production and administrative expenses incurred by entity C. On the basis of this operating model, the arrangement is intended to operate at a break-even level.

From the fact pattern above, the following facts and circumstances are relevant:

- The obligation of the parties to purchase all the output produced by entity C reflects the exclusive dependence of entity C upon the parties for the generation of cash flows and, thus, the parties have an obligation to fund the settlement of the liabilities of entity C.

> - The fact that the parties have rights to all the output produced by entity C means that the parties are consuming, and therefore have rights to, all the economic benefits of the assets of entity C.
>
> These facts and circumstances indicate that the arrangement is a joint operation. The conclusion about the classification of the joint arrangement in these circumstances would not change if, instead of the parties using their share of the output themselves in a subsequent manufacturing process, the parties sold their share of the output to third parties.
>
> If the parties changed the terms of the contractual arrangement so that the arrangement was able to sell output to third parties, this would result in entity C assuming demand, inventory and credit risks. In that scenario, such a change in the facts and circumstances would require reassessment of the classification of the joint arrangement. Such facts and circumstances would indicate that the arrangement is a joint venture.

B33　The following flow chart reflects the assessment an entity follows to classify an arrangement when the joint arrangement is structured through a separate vehicle:

IFRS 11 JOINT ARRANGEMENTS

Classification of a joint arrangement structured through a separate vehicle

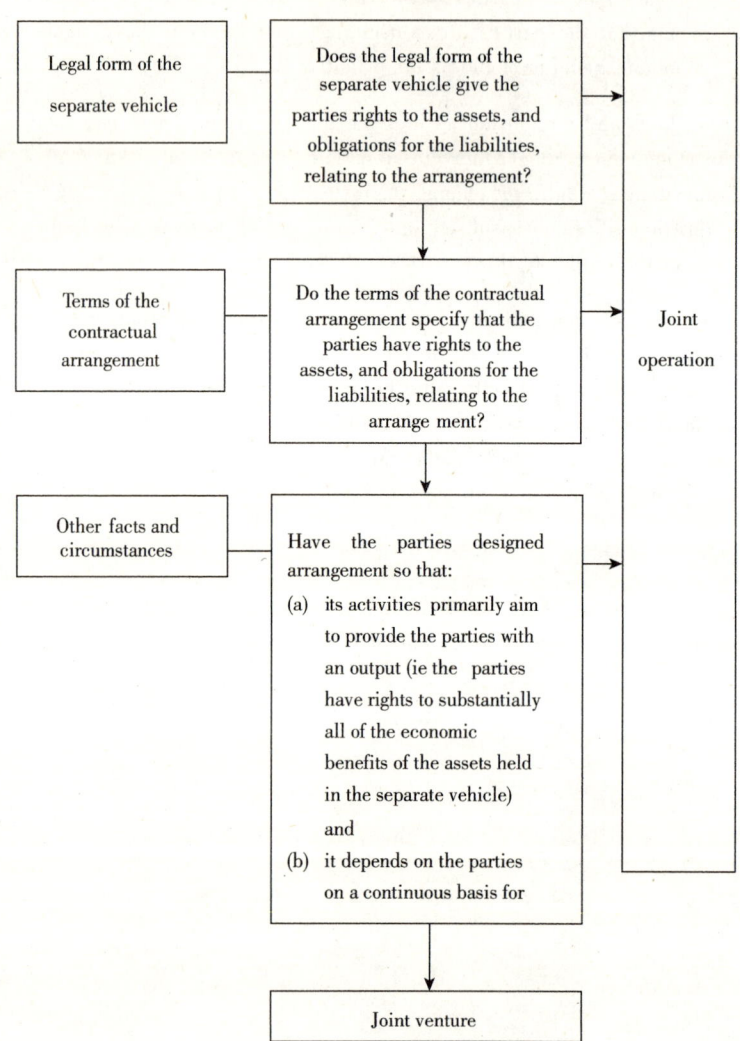

Financial statements of parties to a joint arrangement (paragraph 22)

Accounting for sales or contributions of assets to a joint operation

B34   When an entity enters into a transaction with a joint operation in which it is a joint operator, such as a sale or contribution of assets, it is conducting the transaction with the other parties to the joint operation and, as such, the joint operator shall recognise gains and losses resulting from such a transaction only to the extent of the other parties' interests in the joint operation.

B35   When such transactions provide evidence of a reduction in the net realisable value of the assets to be sold or contributed to the joint operation, or of an impairment loss of those assets, those losses shall be recognised fully by the joint operator.

Accounting for purchases of assets from a joint operation

B36   When an entity enters into a transaction with a joint operation in which it is a joint operator, such as a purchase of assets, it shall not recognise its share of the gains and losses until it resells those assets to a third party.

B37   When such transactions provide evidence of a reduction in the net realisable value of the assets to be purchased or of an impairment loss of those assets, a joint operator shall recognise its share of those losses.

IFRS 11 JOINT ARRANGEMENTS

Appendix C
Effective date, transition and withdrawal of other IFRSs

This appendix is an integral part of the IFRS and has the same authority as the other parts of the IFRS.

Effective date

C1 An entity shall apply this IFRS for annual periods beginning on or after 1 January 2013. Earlier application is permitted. If an entity applies this IFRS earlier, it shall disclose that fact and apply IFRS 10, IFRS 12 *Disclosure of Interests in Other Entities*, IAS 27 (as amended in 2011) and IAS 28 (as amended in 2011) at the same time.

C1A *Consolidated Financial Statements, Joint Arrangements and Disclosure of Interests in Other Entities: Transition Guidance* (Amendments to IFRS 10, IFRS 11 and IFRS 12), issued in June 2012, amended paragraphs C2 – C5, C7 – C10 and C12 and added paragraphs C1B and C12A – C12B. An entity shall apply those amendments for annual periods beginning on or after 1 January 2013. If an entity applies IFRS 11 for an earlier period, it shall apply those amendments for that earlier period.

C1B Notwithstanding the requirements of paragraph 28 of IAS 8 *Accounting Policies, Changes in Accounting Estimates and Errors*, when this IFRS is first applied, an entity need only present the quantitative information required by paragraph 28(f) of IAS 8 for, the annual period immediately preceding the first annual period for which IFRS 11 is applied (the 'immediately preceding period'). An entity may also present this information for the current period or for earlier comparative periods, but is not required to do so.

Transition

Joint ventures—transition from proportionate consolidation to the equity method

C2 When changing from proportionate consolidation to the equity method, an entity shall recognise its investment in the joint venture as at the beginning of the immediately preceding period. That initial investment shall be measured as the aggregate of the carrying amounts of the assets and liabilities that the entity had previously proportionately consolidated, including any goodwill arising from acquisition. If the goodwill previously belonged to a larger cash-generating unit, or to a group of cash-generating units, the entity shall allocate goodwill to the joint venture on the basis of the

C3 The opening balance of the investment determined in accordance with paragraph C2 is regarded as the deemed cost of the investment at initial recognition. An entity shall apply paragraphs 40 – 43 of IAS 28 (as amended in 2011) to the opening balance of the investment to assess whether the investment is impaired and shall recognise any impairment loss as an adjustment to retained earnings at the beginning of the immediately preceding period. The initial recognition exception in paragraphs 15 and 24 of IAS 12 *Income Taxes* does not apply when the entity recognises an investment in a joint venture resulting from applying the transition requirements for joint ventures that had previously been proportionately consolidated.

C4 If aggregating all previously proportionately consolidated assets and liabilities results in negative net assets, an entity shall assess whether it has legal or constructive obligations in relation to the negative net assets and, if so, the entity shall recognise the corresponding liability. If the entity concludes that it does not have legal or constructive obligations in relation to the negative net assets, it shall not recognise the corresponding liability but it shall adjust retained earnings at the beginning of the immediately preceding period. The entity shall disclose this fact, along with its cumulative unrecognised share of losses of its joint ventures as at the beginning of the immediately preceding period and at the date at which this IFRS is first applied.

C5 An entity shall disclose a breakdown of the assets and liabilities that have been aggregated into the single line investment balance as at the beginning of the immediately preceding period. That disclosure shall be prepared in an aggregated manner for all joint ventures for which an entity applies the transition requirements referred to in paragraphs C2 – C6.

C6 After initial recognition, an entity shall account for its investment in the joint venture using the equity method in accordance with IAS 28 (as amended in 2011).

Joint operations—transition from the equity method to accounting for assets and liabilities

C7 When changing from the equity method to accounting for assets and liabilities in respect of its interest in a joint operation, an entity shall, at the beginning of the immediately preceding period, derecognise the investment that was previously accounted for using the equity method and any other items that formed part of the entity's net investment in the arrangement in accordance with paragraph 38 of IAS 28 (as amended in 2011) and recognise its share of each of the assets and the liabilities in respect of its interest in the joint operation, including any goodwill that might have formed part of the carrying amount of the investment.

C8 An entity shall determine its interest in the assets and liabilities relating to the joint operation on the basis of its rights and obligations in a specified proportion in accordance with the contractual arrangement. An entity measures the initial carrying amounts of the assets and liabilities by disaggregating them from the carrying amount of the investment at the beginning of the immediately preceding period on the basis of the information used by the entity in applying the equity method.

C9 Any difference arising from the investment previously accounted for using the equity method together with any other items that formed part of the entity's net investment in the arrangement in accordance with paragraph 38 of IAS 28 (as amended in 2011), and the net amount of the assets and liabilities, including any goodwill, recognised shall be:

(a) offset against any goodwill relating to the investment with any remaining difference adjusted against retained earnings at the beginning of the immediately preceding period, if the net amount of the assets and liabilities, including any goodwill, recognised is higher than the investment (and any other items that formed part of the entity's net investment) derecognised.

(b) adjusted against retained earnings at the beginning of the immediately preceding period, if the net amount of the assets and liabilities, including any goodwill, recognised is lower than the investment (and any other items that formed part of the entity's net investment) derecognised.

C10 An entity changing from the equity method to accounting for assets and liabilities shall provide a reconciliation between the investment derecognised, and the assets and liabilities recognised, together with any remaining difference adjusted against retained earnings, at the beginning of the immediately preceding period.

C11 The initial recognition exception in paragraphs 15 and 24 of IAS 12 does not apply when the entity recognises assets and liabilities relating to its interest in a joint operation.

Transition provisions in an entity's separate financial statements

C12 An entity that, in accordance with paragraph 10 of IAS 27, was previously accounting in its separate financial statements for its interest in a joint operation as an investment at cost or in accordance with IFRS 9 shall:

IFRS 11 JOINT ARRANGEMENTS

(a) derecognise the investment and recognise the assets and the liabilities in respect of its interest in the joint operation at the amounts determined in accordance with paragraphs C7 – C9.

(b) provide a reconciliation between the investment derecognised, and the assets and liabilities recognised, together with any remaining difference adjusted in retained earnings, at the beginning of the immediately preceding period.

C12A Notwithstanding the references to the 'immediately preceding period' in paragraphs C2-C12, an entity may also present adjusted comparative information for any earlier periods presented, but is not required to do so. If an entity does present adjusted comparative information for any earlier periods, all references to the 'immediately preceding period' in paragraphs C2-C12 shall be read as the 'earliest adjusted comparative period presented'.

C12B If an entity presents unadjusted comparative information for any earlier periods, it shall clearly identify the information that has not been adjusted, state that it has been prepared on a different basis, and explain that basis.

C13 The initial recognition exception in paragraphs 15 and 24 of IAS 12 does not apply when the entity recognises assets and liabilities relating to its interest in a joint operation in its separate financial statements resulting from applying the transition requirements for joint operations referred to in paragraph C12.

References to IFRS 9

C14 If an entity applies this IFRS but does not yet apply IFRS 9, any reference to IFRS 9 shall be read as a reference to IAS 39 *Financial Instruments: Recognition and Measurement*.

Withdrawal of other IFRSs

C15 This IFRS supersedes the following IFRSs:

(a) IAS 31 *Interests in Joint Ventures*; and

(b) SIC-13 *Jointly Controlled Entities—Non-Monetary Contributions by Venturers*.

Approval by the Board of IFRS 11 issued in May 2011

International Financial Reporting Standard 11 Joint Arrangements was approved for issue by the fifteen members of the International Accounting Standards Board.

Sir David Tweedie   Chairman
Stephen Cooper
Philippe Danjou
Jan Engström
Patrick Finnegan
Amaro Luiz de Oliveira Gomes
Prabhakar Kalavacherla
Elke König
Patricia McConnell
Warren J McGregor
Paul Pacter
Darrel Scott
John T Smith
Tatsumi Yamada
Wei-Guo Zhang

Basis for Conclusions on
IFRS 11 Joint Arrangements

IFRS 11 JOINT ARRANGEMENTS

CONTENTS

INTRODUCTION	BC1 – BC3
OBJECTIVE	BC4 – BC12
The problems with IAS 31	BC7 – BC8
Improving IAS 31 with the principles of IFRS 11	BC9 – BC12
SCOPE	BC13 – BC18
Scope exception	BC15 – BC18
JOINT ARRANGEMENTS	BC19 – BC23
Joint control	BC20 – BC23
TYPES OF JOINT ARRANGEMENT	BC24 – BC37
FINANCIAL STATEMENTS OF PARTIES TO A JOINT ARRANGEMENT	BC38 – BC51
Joint operation	BC38 – BC40
Joint venture	BC41 – BC45
Transactions between an entity and a joint operation in which that entity is a joint operator and incorporation of SIC-13 into the IFRS	BC46 – BC47
Reporting interests in joint arrangements in the financial statements of parties that participate in, but do not have joint control of, a joint arrangement	BC48 – BC50
Joint operation held for sale	BC51
DISCLOSURE	BC52 – BC55
EFFECTIVE DATE	BC56 – BC59
TRANSITION	BC60 – BC69
SUMMARY OF MAIN CHANGES FROM ED 9	BC70
COST-BENEFIT CONSIDERATIONS	BC71 – BC78

IFRS 11 JOINT ARRANGEMENTS

This Basis for Conclusions accompanies, but is not part of, IFRS 11.

Introduction

BC1　This Basis for Conclusions summarises the International Accounting Standards Board's considerations in reaching the conclusions in IFRS 11 *Joint Arrangements*. Individual Board members gave greater weight to some factors than to others.

BC2　The Board added the joint ventures project to its agenda as part of the project to reduce differences between International Financial Reporting Standards (IFRSs) and US generally accepted accounting principles (GAAP). The requirements of IFRS 11 were not deliberated by the US Financial Accounting Standards Board (FASB).

BC3　The Board focused its deliberations on enhancing the faithful representation of joint arrangements that an entity provides in its financial statements, by establishing a principle-based approach to accounting for joint arrangements, and by requiring enhanced disclosures. Even though the Board focused its efforts on improving the reporting of joint arrangements, the result is that the requirements of the IFRS achieve closer convergence with US GAAP than did IAS 31 *Interests in Joint Ventures*, which IFRS 11 supersedes.

Objective

BC4　IFRS 11 sets out requirements for the recognition and measurement of an entity's interest in joint arrangements. The requirements for the disclosure of an entity's interest in joint arrangements have been included in IFRS 12 *Disclosure of Interests in Other Entities* (see paragraphs BC52 – BC55). IFRS 11 is concerned principally with addressing two aspects of IAS 31 that the Board regarded as impediments to high quality reporting of joint arrangements: first, that the structure of the arrangement was the only determinant of the accounting, and second, that an entity had a choice of accounting treatment for interests in jointly controlled entities.

BC5　The Board did not reconsider all the requirements in IAS 31. For example, the Board did not reconsider the equity method. Accordingly, this Basis for Conclusions does not discuss requirements of IAS 31 that the Board did not reconsider.

BC6　The Board published its proposals in an exposure draft, ED 9 *Joint Arrangements*, in September 2007 with a comment deadline of 11 January 2008. The Board received over 110 comment letters on the exposure draft.

The problems with IAS 31

BC7 IAS 31 established different accounting requirements depending on whether the arrangements were structured through an entity. Jointly controlled operations and jointly controlled assets were arrangements that did not require the establishment of an entity or financial structure that is separate from the parties. IAS 31 required parties to these arrangements to recognise assets, liabilities, revenues and expenses arising from the arrangements. When arrangements were structured through an entity, IAS 31 classified them as jointly controlled entities. Parties with interests in jointly controlled entities accounted for them using proportionate consolidation or, as an alternative, the equity method.

BC8 The problem with basing different accounting requirements solely on the existence of an entity, combined with the choice of accounting treatment for jointly controlled entities, was that some arrangements that gave the parties similar rights and obligations were accounted for differently and, conversely, arrangements that gave the parties different rights and obligations were accounted for similarly. The Board's policy is to exclude options in accounting treatment from accounting standards whenever possible. Such options can lead to similar transactions being accounted for in different ways and, therefore, can impair comparability.

Improving IAS 31 with the principles of IFRS 11

BC9 In the Board's view, the accounting for joint arrangements should reflect the rights and obligations that the parties have as a result of their interests in the arrangements, regardless of those arrangements' structure or legal form. This is the principle that IFRS 11 establishes for parties to a joint arrangement when accounting for their interests in the arrangements. However, the Board acknowledges that sometimes the structure or the legal form of the joint arrangements is decisive in determining the parties' rights and obligations arising from the arrangements and, consequently, in determining the classification of the joint arrangements (see paragraphs BC26 and BC31).

BC10 Entities applying IAS 31 were required to choose the same accounting treatment (ie proportionate consolidation or equity method) when accounting for all of their interests in jointly controlled entities. Applying the same accounting treatment to all the interests that an entity has in different jointly controlled entities might not always lead to the faithful representation of each of those interests. For example, an entity whose policy was to account for all of its interests in jointly controlled entities using proportionate consolidation might have recognised assets and liabilities proportionately even though this did not faithfully represent the entity's rights and obligations in the assets and liabilities of particular joint arrangements. Conversely, an entity might have accounted for all of its interests in jointly controlled entities using the equity method, when the recognition of the entity's rights and obligations in particular joint arrangements would instead have led to the recognition of assets and liabilities.

BC11 The accounting for joint arrangements required by the IFRS is not a function of an entity's accounting policy choice but is, instead, determined by an entity applying the principles of the IFRS to each of its joint arrangements and recognising, as a result, the rights and obligations arising from each of them. The Board concluded that proportionate consolidation is not an appropriate method to account for interests in joint arrangements when the parties have neither rights to the assets, nor obligations for the liabilities, relating to the arrangement. The Board also concluded that the equity method is not an appropriate method to account for interests in joint arrangements when parties have rights to the assets, and obligations for the liabilities, relating to the arrangement. The Board believes that it is misleading for users of financial statements if an entity recognises assets and liabilities for which it does not have rights or obligations, or does not recognise assets and liabilities for which it does have rights and obligations.

BC12 The Board also reconsidered the disclosure requirements in IAS 31 for interests in joint arrangements. The Board believes that the disclosure requirements in IFRS 12 will enable users to gain a better understanding of the nature and extent of an entity's operations undertaken through joint arrangements.

Scope

BC13 The IFRS should be applied by all entities that are a party to a joint arrangement. The IFRS does not change the two essential characteristics that IAS 31 required arrangements to have in order to be deemed 'joint ventures', ie that a contractual arrangement that binds the parties to the arrangement exists, and that the contractual arrangement establishes that two or more of those parties have joint control of the arrangement.

BC14 The Board believes that the new definition of control and the application requirements to assess control in IFRS 10 *Consolidated Financial Statements* will assist entities in determining whether an arrangement is controlled or jointly controlled, and in that respect it might cause entities to reconsider their previous assessment of their relationship with the investee. Despite the changes that these reassessments might cause, the Board believes that arrangements that were within the scope of IAS 31 would generally also be within the scope of IFRS 11.

Scope exception

BC15 The Board reconsidered the scope exception of IAS 31 that had also been proposed in ED 9. The Board concluded that the scope exception in ED 9 for interests in joint ventures held by venture capital organisations, or mutual funds, unit trusts and similar entities, including investment-linked insurance funds, that are measured at fair value through profit or loss in accordance with IFRS 9 *Financial Instruments*, is more appropriately characterised as a measurement exemption, not as a scope exception.

BC16 The Board observed that when venture capital organisations, or mutual funds, unit trusts and similar entities, including investment-linked insurance funds, conclude that they have an interest in a joint arrangement, this is because the arrangement has the characteristics of a joint arrangement as specified in IFRS 11 (ie a contractual arrangement exists that establishes that two or more parties have joint control of the arrangement).

BC17 The Board also observed that the scope exception in ED 9 did not relate to the fact that these arrangements do not have the characteristics of joint arrangements, but to the fact that for investments held by venture capital organisations, or mutual funds, unit trusts and similar entities, including investment-linked insurance funds, fair value measurement provides more useful information for users of the financial statements than would application of the equity method.

BC18 Accordingly, the Board decided to maintain the option that permits such entities to measure their interests in joint ventures at fair value through profit or loss in accordance with IFRS 9, but clarified that this is an exemption from the requirement to measure interests in joint ventures using the equity method, rather than an exception to the scope of IFRS 11 for joint ventures in which these entities have interests.

Joint arrangements

BC19 The Board decided to use the term 'joint arrangement', rather than 'joint venture', to describe arrangements that are subject to the requirements of the IFRS. As noted in paragraph BC13, the IFRS does not change the two essential characteristics that IAS 31 required for arrangements to be 'joint ventures': a contractual arrangement that binds the parties to the arrangement exists, and the contractual arrangement establishes that two or more of those parties have joint control of the arrangement.

Joint control

BC20 In ED 9, the proposed definition of 'joint arrangement' required 'shared decision-making' by all the parties to the arrangement. Some respondents questioned how 'shared decision-making' was intended to operate and how it differed from 'joint control'. The Board introduced the term 'shared decision-making' in the exposure draft instead of 'joint control' because control was defined in IAS 27 *Consolidated and Separate Financial Statements* in the context of having power over the financial and operating policies of an entity. ① During its redeliberation of ED 9, the Board concluded that in joint arrangements, it is the activity undertaken by the parties that is the matter over which the parties share control or share decision-making, regardless of whether the activity is conducted in a separate entity. Consequently, the Board concluded that 'joint control' is a term that expresses better than 'shared decision-making' that the control of the activity that is the subject matter of the arrangement is shared among the parties with joint control of the arrangement.

BC21 The Board did not reconsider the concept of 'joint control' as defined in IAS 31 or in ED 9 (ie the requirement of unanimous consent for the decisions that give the parties control of an arrangement). However, the definition of 'joint control' in the IFRS is different from those in IAS 31 and ED 9. The reason for the change is to align the definition of 'joint control' with the definition of 'control' in IFRS 10. IFRS 11 directs parties to an arrangement to assess first whether all the parties, or a group of the parties, control the arrangement collectively, on the basis of the definition of control and corresponding guidance in IFRS 10. Once an entity has concluded that the arrangement is collectively controlled by all the parties, or by a group of the parties, joint control exists only when decisions about the activities that significantly affect the returns of the arrangement (ie the relevant activities) require the unanimous consent of those parties.

BC22 In response to concerns expressed by some respondents who pointed out that, unlike IAS 31, ED 9 did not include the term 'investors in a joint arrangement', the Board clarified during its redeliberation of ED 9 that not all the parties to a joint arrangement need to have joint control for the arrangement to be a joint arrangement. Indeed, some of the parties to a joint arrangement can have joint control whereas others, although able to participate, do not have joint control of the arrangement. The Board decided to use the terms 'joint operators' to designate parties with joint control of a 'joint operation' and 'joint venturers' to designate parties with joint control of a 'joint venture' (see

---

① The consolidation requirements in IAS 27 were replaced by IFRS 10 *Consolidated Financial Statements* issued in 2011 and the definition of control was revised.

paragraph BC24).

BC23 The Board observed that the parties to a joint arrangement might agree to change or modify the governance and decision-making process of the arrangement at any time. As a result of such a change, a party might gain or lose joint control of the arrangement. Consequently, the Board concluded that if facts and circumstances change, the parties to a joint arrangement should reassess whether they are parties with joint control of the arrangement.

Types of joint arrangement

BC24 The IFRS classifies joint arrangements into two types—'joint operations' and 'joint ventures'. Parties with joint control of a joint operation have rights to the assets, and obligations for the liabilities, relating to the arrangement ('joint operators'), whereas parties with joint control of a joint venture ('joint venturers') have rights to the net assets of the arrangement.

BC25 The classification of joint arrangements into two types was considered by the Board in its redeliberation of the exposure draft. ED 9 proposed to classify joint arrangements into three types—'joint operations', 'joint assets' and 'joint ventures'. The Board observed that in some instances it might be difficult to assess whether an arrangement is a 'joint operation' or a 'joint asset'. This is because elements from both types of joint arrangement are sometimes present (in many arrangements joint assets are also jointly operated, and therefore such arrangements could be viewed as a 'joint asset' or as a 'joint operation'). Additionally, both types of joint arrangement result in the same accounting outcome (ie recognition of assets and liabilities and corresponding revenues and expenses). For these reasons, the Board decided to merge 'joint operations' and 'joint assets' into a single type of joint arrangement called 'joint operation'. This decision simplifies the IFRS by aligning the two types of joint arrangement presented by the IFRS (ie 'joint operations' and 'joint ventures') with the two possible accounting outcomes (ie recognition of assets, liabilities, revenues and expenses, or recognition of an investment accounted for using the equity method).

BC26 The Board observed that when the parties do not structure their joint arrangement through a separate vehicle (ie arrangements that were formerly 'jointly controlled operations' and 'jointly controlled assets' in IAS 31), the parties determine in the contractual arrangements their rights to the assets, and their obligations for the liabilities, relating to the arrangement. Such arrangements are joint operations.

BC27 In reaching this conclusion, the Board acknowledged the possibility that parties to a joint arrangement that is not structured through a separate vehicle might establish terms in the contractual arrangement under which the parties have rights only to the net assets of the arrangement. The Board thought that this possibility was likely to be rare and that the benefits of introducing an additional assessment in the classification of joint arrangements when these are not structured through separate vehicles would not outweigh the costs of increasing the complexity of the IFRS. This is because in the vast majority of cases, accounting for joint arrangements that are not structured through separate vehicles on a gross basis leads to the faithful representation of the parties' rights and obligations arising from those arrangements.

BC28   The Board acknowledged that classifying jointly controlled entities in IAS 31 into joint operations or joint ventures in the IFRS requires an entity to assess its rights and obligations arising from these arrangements, which will require the entity to exercise judgement.

BC29   The Board considered whether the definition of a 'business', as defined in IFRS 3 *Business Combinations*, would be helpful in distinguishing between a joint venture and a joint operation. Because a 'business' can be found in all types of joint arrangement, the Board decided not to pursue this approach.

BC30   The Board also concluded that there should not be a rebuttable presumption that the arrangement is a joint venture when it has been structured through a separate vehicle. The Board decided that parties to a joint arrangement that is structured through a separate vehicle should assess the classification of the arrangement by taking into consideration all facts and circumstances. The Board noted that an entity should take into consideration the legal form of the separate vehicle, the terms agreed in the contractual arrangement and, when relevant, any other facts and circumstances.

BC31   In taking this approach, the Board observed that the legal form of the separate vehicle in which the joint arrangement is structured provides an initial indicator of the parties' rights to the assets, and obligations for the liabilities, relating to the arrangement. The exception is when the legal form of the separate vehicle does not confer separation between the parties and the vehicle. In such a case, the Board concluded that the assessment of the rights and obligations conferred upon the parties by the legal form of that separate vehicle would be sufficient to conclude that the arrangement is a joint operation.

BC32   The Board believes that the selection of a particular legal form is in many cases driven by the intended economic substance that the particular legal form delivers. However, the Board observed that in some cases the choice of a particular legal form responds to tax,

IFRS 11 JOINT ARRANGEMENTS

regulatory requirements or other reasons that can alter the intended economic substance initially sought by the parties to the arrangement. In those instances, the parties might use their contractual arrangements to modify the effects that the legal form of the arrangement would otherwise have on their rights and obligations.

BC33　The Board noted that other facts and circumstances might also affect the rights and obligations of the parties to a joint arrangement and, ultimately, affect the classification of the arrangement. Therefore, the parties should recognise the assets and liabilities relating to an arrangement if the parties designed the arrangement so that its activities primarily aimed to provide the parties with an output (ie the parties are entitled to substantially all the economic benefits of the assets relating to the arrangement) and they are, as a result of the design of the arrangement, obliged to settle the liabilities relating to the arrangement.

BC34　The IFRS defines 'joint ventures' as arrangements whereby the parties that have joint control of the arrangement (ie the joint venturers) have rights to the net assets of the arrangement. The Board observed that the term 'net assets' in the definition of joint ventures aimed to portray that the joint venturers have rights to an investment in the arrangement. However, such a definition (ie 'rights to the net assets of the arrangement') would not prevent a joint venturer from having a net liability position arising from its involvement in the joint venture. This could happen, for example, if the joint venture had incurred losses that had reduced the joint venturer's investment to zero, and as a result of the joint venturer having provided a guarantee to cover any losses that the joint venture might incur, the joint venturer has an obligation for those losses. The Board observed that neither the provision of the guarantee by the joint venturer, nor the liability assumed by the joint venturer as a result of the joint venture incurring losses, determines that the arrangement is a joint operation.

BC35　Many respondents to ED 9 were concerned that joint ventures could be merely 'residuals'. This is because these respondents interpreted joint ventures to mean that after parties had identified rights to individual assets or obligations for expenses or financing, joint ventures would be merely any remaining assets and liabilities of the arrangement. As a result of these concerns, the Board clarified that the unit of account of a joint arrangement is the activity that two or more parties have agreed to control jointly, and that a party should assess its rights to the assets, and obligations for the liabilities, relating to that activity. Consequently, the term 'joint venture' refers to a jointly controlled activity in which the parties have an investment.

BC36　During its redeliberation of ED 9, the Board made it clear that different joint arrangements or different types of joint arrangement can be established beneath the umbrella of a single arrangement or framework agreement to deal with, for example, different activities that are interrelated. The Board also observed the possibility that within the same separate vehicle the parties may undertake different activities in which they have different rights to the assets, and obligations for the liabilities, relating to these different activities resulting in different types of joint arrangement conducted within the same separate vehicle. However, the Board acknowledged that even though this situation is conceptually possible, it would be rare in practice.

BC37 The Board observed that the rights and obligations of parties to joint arrangements might change over time. This might happen, for example, as a result of a change in the purpose of the arrangement that might trigger a reconsideration of the terms of the contractual arrangements. Consequently, the Board concluded that the assessment of the type of joint arrangement needs to be a continuous process, to the extent that facts and circumstances change.

Financial statements of parties to a joint arrangement

Joint operation

BC38 In relation to the accounting for a party's interest in a joint operation, some respondents to ED 9 enquired how proportionate consolidation differed from the recognition of (or recognition of shares of) assets, liabilities, revenues and expenses arising from a joint operation. The Board noted that there are two main differences between recognising assets, liabilities, revenues and expenses relating to the activity of the joint operation and proportionate consolidation. The first difference relates to the fact that the rights and obligations, as specified in the contractual arrangement, that an entity has with respect to the assets, liabilities, revenues and expenses relating to a joint operation might differ from its ownership interest in the joint operation. The IFRS requires an entity with an interest in a joint operation to recognise assets, liabilities, revenues and expenses according to the entity's shares in the assets, liabilities, revenues and expenses of the joint operation as determined and specified in the contractual arrangement, rather than basing the recognition of assets, liabilities, revenues and expenses on the ownership interest that the entity has in the joint operation. The second difference from proportionate consolidation is that the parties' interests in a joint operation are recognised in their separate financial statements. Consequently, there is no difference in what is recognised in the parties' separate financial statements and the parties' consolidated financial statements or the parties' financial statements in which investments are accounted for using the equity method.

BC39 Respondents also suggested that the IFRS should provide more clarity in stating the requirements for the accounting for shares of assets in joint operations. Many respondents to ED 9 were not clear whether parties to a joint operation that had rights to the assets should recognise a 'right to use' or a 'right to a share' or whether they should instead directly recognise 'their share of the joint assets, classified according to the nature of the asset'. The concern raised by this uncertainty was the different accounting implications of these interpretations —ie accounting for rights or accounting for shares of assets. The Board concluded that a party to a joint operation should recognise its assets or its share of any assets in accordance with the IFRSs applicable to the particular assets.

BC40 An additional concern raised by some respondents to ED 9 was how the unit of account relating to the share of assets and liabilities to be accounted for by the parties to a joint operation should be delineated. The Board observed that ED 9 had not been intended to change this aspect of IAS 31, where the 'share' is determined in accordance with the contractual arrangement. The Board concluded that the contractual arrangement generally delineates the 'share' or 'part' not only of the assets or liabilities of the parties to joint operations, but also of their 'share' of any revenues and expenses arising from the joint operation.

Joint venture

BC41 In relation to the accounting for interests in joint ventures, the Board decided that entities should recognise their interests using the equity method in accordance with IAS 28 *Investments in Associates and Joint Ventures*, unless the entity is exempted from applying the equity method as stated in that standard. In reaching that conclusion, the Board considered the views of some respondents to ED 9 who pointed out that joint control and significant influence are different. Proponents of this view argue that it is not appropriate to account for an associate and a joint venture in the same way using the equity method. Although the Board acknowledged that significant influence and joint control are different, the Board concluded that, except for specific circumstances that are addressed in IAS 28 (as amended in 2011), the equity method is the most appropriate method to account for joint ventures because it is a method that accounts for an entity's interest in the net assets of an investee. Reconsideration of the equity method was outside the scope of the joint ventures project.

BC42 Other respondents expressed concerns about the elimination of proportionate consolidation. Those respondents believe that proportionate consolidation more faithfully represents the economic substance of the arrangements, and better meets the information needs of users of financial statements. The Board acknowledged these concerns, but observed that the approach in the IFRS is consistent with its view of what constitutes the economic substance of an entity's interests in joint arrangements, a view that it concedes may differ from that of those respondents. This seems inevitable given that, the evidence suggests that in accounting for interests in jointly controlled entities approximately half of the entities applying IFRSs use proportionate consolidation and half use the equity method. The variation in practice, which is facilitated by the option in IAS 31, is a prime motivation for developing IFRS 11 (see paragraphs BC7 and BC8). That variation will, inevitably, be a source of disagreement.

BC43 The Board believes that the accounting for joint arrangements should faithfully reflect the rights and obligations that the parties have in respect of the assets and liabilities relating to the arrangement. In that respect, the Board observes that the activities that are the subject of different joint arrangements might be operationally very similar, but that the contractual terms agreed by the parties to these joint arrangements might confer on the parties very different rights to the assets, and obligations for the liabilities, relating to such activities. Consequently, the Board believes that the economic substance of the arrangements does not depend exclusively on whether the activities undertaken through joint arrangements are closely related to the activities undertaken by the parties on their own, or on whether the parties are closely involved in the operations of the arrangements. Instead, the economic substance of the arrangements depends on the rights and obligations assumed by the parties when carrying out such activities. It is those rights and obligations that the accounting for joint arrangements should reflect.

BC44 The Board observes that the IFRS requires parties to account for assets and liabilities when the contractual arrangement specifies that they have rights to the assets and obligations for the liabilities. The Board believes that accounting for joint arrangements that is based on the principles of the IFRS will contribute not only to improving the faithful representation of an entity's interests in joint arrangements, but also to enhancing comparability. This is because arrangements in which the parties have rights to the assets and obligations for the liabilities will require the same accounting treatment. In the same way, arrangements in which the parties have rights to the net assets of the arrangement will also require the same accounting treatment.

BC45 The Board does not believe that the elimination of proportionate consolidation will cause a loss of information for users of financial statements. This is because the disclosure requirements in IFRS 12, when compared with IAS 31, will improve the quality of the information provided to users relating to an entity's interest in joint ventures. The disclosure requirements in IFRS 12 will provide users with information about individual joint ventures when those joint ventures are material to the reporting entity. In addition, the Board notes that the summarised financial information required in IFRS 12 results in a higher degree of detail than did IAS 31, which gives users a better basis for assessing the effect on the reporting entity of the activities carried out through joint ventures.

Transactions between an entity and a joint operation in which that entity is a joint operator and incorporation of SIC-13 into the IFRS

BC46　In its redeliberation of ED 9, the Board noted that the exposure draft was silent on the accounting for transactions between an entity and a joint operation in which that entity is a joint operator. The Board observed that the IFRS did not aim to change the accounting procedures that entities applied when accounting for such transactions in accordance with IAS 31, but it did acknowledge that the IFRS should state what those requirements were.

BC47　The Board also decided to include the requirements for the accounting for transactions entered into between a joint venturer and a joint venture, including the consensus of SIC-13 *Jointly Controlled Entities—Non-Monetary Contributions by Venturers*, in IAS 28 (as amended in 2011).

Reporting interests in joint arrangements in the financial statements of parties that participate in, but do not have joint control of, a joint arrangement

BC48　The Board decided to clarify in the IFRS that an arrangement can be a joint arrangement even though not all of its parties have joint control of the arrangement. This was consistent with IAS 31, which defined an 'investor in a joint venture' as a party to a joint venture that does not have joint control of that joint venture. The Board noted, however, that relating the term 'investor' exclusively to parties with no joint control of the arrangement can be confusing because the parties with joint control of the arrangement are also investors in those arrangements. Accordingly, the Board modified the language in the IFRS to avoid that confusion. However, even though in its redeliberation of ED 9 the Board highlighted that the IFRS establishes recognition and measurement requirements for the parties with joint control of a joint arrangement, the Board decided to address the accounting requirements for parties that participate in, but do not have joint control of, a joint arrangement, to reduce divergence in practice.

BC49　In relation to parties that participate in, but do not have joint control of, a joint arrangement that is a joint operation, the Board focused its discussions on those parties for which the contractual arrangements specify that they have rights to the assets, and obligations for the liabilities, relating to the joint operation. The Board concluded that, even though those parties are not joint operators, they do have rights and obligations for the assets, liabilities, revenues and expenses relating to the joint operation, which they should recognise in accordance with the terms of the contractual arrangement.

BC50 The Board considered that the requirements in IAS 31 for parties that participate in, but do not have joint control of, joint ventures were appropriate and therefore decided to carry them forward to the IFRS. Consequently, such a party should account for its investment in accordance with IFRS 9 or, if that party has significant influence over the joint venture, in accordance with IAS 28 (as amended in 2011).

Joint operation held for sale

BC51 ED 9 was silent on how an entity should account for an interest in a joint operation that is classified as held for sale. The Board decided that a joint operator should account for an interest in a joint operation that is classified as held for sale in accordance with IFRS 5 *Non-current Assets Held for Sale and Discontinued Operations*. The Board also confirmed that the guidance in IFRS 5 for the classification of a disposal group as held for sale would apply to interests in joint operations held for sale.

Disclosure

BC52 As part of its redeliberation of ED 9 and ED 10 *Consolidated Financial Statements*, the Board identified an opportunity to integrate and make consistent the disclosure requirements for subsidiaries, joint arrangements, associates and unconsolidated structured entities, and to present those requirements in a single IFRS.

BC53 The Board observed that IAS 27 (as revised in 2003), IAS 28 (as revised in 2003) and IAS 31 contained many similar disclosure requirements. ED 9 had already proposed amendments to the disclosure requirements for joint ventures and associates to align the disclosure requirements for those two types of investments more closely. The Board noted that the majority of respondents agreed with the proposals in ED 9 to align the disclosures for joint ventures with the disclosures in IAS 28 for associates.

BC54 As a result, the Board combined the disclosure requirements for interest with subsidiaries, joint arrangements, associates and unconsolidated structured entities within a single comprehensive standard, IFRS 12.

BC55 The Basis for Conclusions accompanying IFRS 12 summarises the Board's considerations in developing that IFRS, including its review of responses to the disclosure proposals in ED 9. Accordingly, IFRS 11 does not include disclosure requirements and this Basis for Conclusions does not incorporate the Board's considerations of responses to the proposed disclosure requirements in ED 9.

Effective date

BC56 The Board decided to align the effective date for the IFRS with the effective date for IFRS 10, IFRS 12, IAS 27 *Separate Financial Statements* and IAS 28 (as amended in 2011). When making this decision, the Board noted that the five IFRSs all deal with the assessment of, and related accounting and disclosure requirements about, a reporting entity's special relationships with other entities (ie when the reporting entity has control or joint control of, or significant influence over, another entity). As a result, the Board concluded that applying IFRS 11 without also applying the other four IFRSs could cause unwarranted confusion.

BC57 The Board usually sets an effective date of between twelve and eighteen months after issuing an IFRS. When deciding the effective date for those IFRSs, the Board considered the following factors:

(a) the time that many countries require for translation and for introducing the mandatory requirements into law.

(b) the consolidation project was related to the global financial crisis that started in 2007 and was accelerated by the Board in response to urgent requests from the leaders of the G20, the Financial Stability Board, users of financial statements, regulators and others to improve the accounting and disclosure of an entity's 'off balance sheet' activities.

(c) the comments received from respondents to the Request for Views *Effective Date and Transition Methods* that was published in October 2010 regarding implementation costs, effective date and transition requirements of the IFRSs to be issued in 2011. Most respondents did not identify the consolidation and joint arrangements IFRSs as having a high impact in terms of the time and resources that their implementation would require. In addition, only a few respondents commented that the effective dates of those IFRSs should be aligned with those of the other IFRSs to be issued in 2011.

BC58 With those factors in mind, the Board decided to require entities to apply the five IFRSs for annual periods beginning on or after 1 January 2013.

BC59 Most respondents to the Request for Views supported early application of the IFRSs to be issued in 2011. Respondents stressed that early application was especially important for first-time adopters in 2011 and 2012. The Board was persuaded by these arguments and decided to permit early application of IFRS 11 but only if an entity applies it in conjunction with the other IFRSs (ie IFRS 10, IFRS 12, IAS 27 (as amended in 2011) and IAS 28 (as amended in 2011)) to avoid a lack of comparability among financial statements, and for the reasons noted in paragraph BC56 that triggered the Board's decision to set the same effective date for all five IFRSs. Even though an entity should apply the five IFRSs at the same time, the Board noted that an entity should not be prevented from providing any information required by IFRS 12 early if by doing so users gained a better understanding of the entity's relationships with other entities.

Transition

BC60　The exposure draft proposed retrospective application of the requirements. In its redeliberation of ED 9, the Board observed that entities affected by the changes introduced by the IFRS would have enough time to prepare to apply the new requirements retrospectively. The Board was informed of a few cases in which entities, on the basis of their analysis of the proposals in ED 9, had already changed their accounting for interests in joint arrangements retrospectively, taking advantage of the accounting option that IAS 31 offered to jointly controlled entities.

BC61　However, in its discussions, the Board considered the views of some respondents to ED 9 who had expressed their concern about applying the requirements retrospectively, because of undue cost and effort. In response to these concerns, the Board decided that in the case of changing from proportionate consolidation to the equity method, an entity should not adjust retrospectively any differences between the accounting methods of proportionate consolidation and equity method, but should instead aggregate the carrying amounts of the assets and liabilities, including any goodwill arising from acquisition, that the entity had previously proportionately consolidated into a single line investment as at the beginning of the earliest period presented.

BC62　The Board also decided that the opening balance of the investment should be tested for impairment in accordance with paragraphs 40 – 43 of IAS 28 (as amended in 2011), with any resulting impairment loss being adjusted against retained earnings at the beginning of the earliest period presented.

BC63　The Board also considered the case when an arrangement that was previously proportionately consolidated has a negative net asset position on transition. In such a case, an entity should assess whether it has legal or constructive obligations in relation to those negative net assets. The Board concluded that if the entity does not have legal or constructive obligations in relation to the negative net assets, it should not recognise the corresponding liability but it should adjust retained earnings at the beginning of the earliest period presented. The entity should also be required to disclose this fact along with its cumulative unrecognised share of losses of the joint venture as at the beginning of the earliest period presented and at the date at which the IFRS is first applied.

BC64 The Board also considered requiring disclosures to help users of financial statements to understand the consequences of the accounting change for those joint arrangements that would be changing from proportionate consolidation to the equity method. To address this need, the Board decided that an entity should disclose a breakdown of the assets and liabilities that have been aggregated into the single line investment as at the beginning of the earliest period presented.

BC65 The Board redeliberated the transition requirements for entities changing from the equity method to accounting for assets and liabilities in respect of their interest in a joint operation. The Board decided to require an entity to recognise each of the assets, including any goodwill arising from acquisition, and the liabilities relating to its interest in the joint operation at its carrying amount on the basis of the information used by the entity in applying the equity method, instead of requiring the entity to remeasure its share of each of those assets and liabilities at the date of transition. The Board did not believe that the costs of requiring entities to remeasure the assets and liabilities relating to the joint operation as a result of the accounting change would outweigh the benefits.

BC66 The Board observed that changing from the equity method to accounting for assets and liabilities in respect of an entity's interest in a joint operation could result in the net amount of the assets and liabilities recognised being either higher or lower than the investment (and any other items that formed part of the entity's net investment in the arrangement) derecognised. In the first case, the Board noted that assets and liabilities recognised could be higher than the investment derecognised when the entity had previously impaired the carrying amount of the investment. The Board observed that, in accordance with IAS 28 (as amended in 2011), such an impairment loss would not have been allocated to any asset, including goodwill, that formed part of the carrying amount of the investment and that as a result, the net amount of the underlying assets and liabilities could be higher than the carrying amount of the investment. To address this, the Board concluded that in such a case, an entity should first adjust the difference against any goodwill related to the investment, with any remaining difference adjusted against retained earnings at the beginning of the earliest period presented. In the second case, the Board noted that the net amount of the assets and liabilities recognised could be lower than the investment derecognised when, for example, an entity applied the same percentage interest to all the underlying assets and liabilities of its investee when determining the carrying amount of its investment using the equity method. However, for some of those underlying assets the entity could have a lower interest when accounting for it as a joint operation. The Board concluded that in such a case, an entity should adjust any difference between the net amount of the assets and liabilities recognised and the investment (and any other items that formed part of the entity's net investment in the arrangement) derecognised against retained earnings at the beginning of the earliest period presented.

BC67 The Board also redeliberated the transition requirements for entities accounting for an interest in a joint operation in its separate financial statements when the entity had previously accounted for this interest at cost or in accordance with IFRS 9. As stated in paragraph BC38, the Board observed that the parties' interests in a joint operation are recognised in their separate financial statements, resulting in no difference between what is recognised in the parties' separate financial statements and in the parties' consolidated financial statements. The Board decided that an entity should adjust any difference between the investment derecognised and the assets and liabilities recognised in respect of the entity's interest in a joint operation against retained earnings at the beginning of the earliest period presented.

BC68 The Board also considered requiring disclosures to help users of financial statements to understand the consequences of the accounting change from the equity method to accounting for assets and liabilities, and when accounting for an interest in a joint operation in the separate financial statements of an entity when the entity had previously accounted for this interest at cost or in accordance with IFRS 9. The Board decided that in both cases, an entity should provide a reconciliation between the investment derecognised and the breakdown of the assets and liabilities recognised, together with any remaining difference adjusted against retained earnings, at the beginning of the earliest period presented.

BC69 As stated in paragraph BC57, respondents to the Request for Views also commented on the transition requirements of the IFRSs to be issued in 2011. In relation to the transition requirements relating to the consolidation and joint arrangements IFRSs, the Board noted that the majority of the respondents to the Request for Views had agreed with the tentative decisions that the Board had previously made at the time of the consultation on the transition requirements for those IFRSs.

BC69A In June 2012, the Board amended the transition guidance in Appendix C to IFRS 10 *Consolidated Financial Statements*. When making those amendments, the Board decided to limit the requirement to present adjusted comparatives to the annual period

IFRS 11 JOINT ARRANGEMENTS

immediately preceding the date of initial application of IFRS 10. This is consistent with the minimum comparative disclosure requirements contained in IAS 1 *Presentation of Finandal Statements* as amended by *Annual Improvements to IFRSs* 2009 – 2011 *Cycle* (issued May 2012). Those amendments confirmed that when an entity applies a changed accounting policy retrospectively, it shall present, as a minimum, three statements of financial position(ie 1 January 2012, 31 December 2012 and 31 December 2013 for a calendar – year entity, assuming no early application of this IFRS) and two of each of the other statements (IAS 1 paragraphs 40A – 40B). Notwithstanding this requirement, the Board confirmed that an entity is not prohibited from presenting adjusted comparative information for earlier periods. The Board also decided to make similar amendments to the transition guidance in Appendix C to this IFRS and Appendix C to IFRS 12 *Disclosure ofInterests in Other Entities* to be consistent with this decision. The Board noted that if all comparative periods are not adjusted then entities should be required to state that fact, clearly identify the information that has not been adj usted, and explain the basis on which it has been prepared.

BC69B The Board also considered the disclosure requirements of IAS 8 *Accounting Policies, Changes in Accounting Estimates and Errors*. On the initial application of an IFRS, paragraph 28(f) of nS 8 requires an entity to disclose, for the current period and for each prior period presented, the amount of any adi ustment for each financial statement line item affected. Changes in the accounting for a j oint arrangement on transition to IFRS 11 are likely to affect many line items throughout the financial statements. The Board agreed that this requirement would be burdensome for preparers and so agreed to limit the disclosure of the quantitative impact of any changes in the accounting for a joint arrangement to only the annual period immediately preceding the first annual period for which IFRS 11 is applied. An entity may also present this information for the current period or for earlier comparative periods, but is not required to do so.

Summary of main changes from ED 9

BC70 The main changes from the exposure draft ED 9 are:

(a) IFRS 11 applies to all entities that have an interest in a joint arrangement. The scope exception in the exposure draft for venture capital organisations, or mutual funds, unit trusts and similar entities, including investment-linked insurance funds, has been removed and has been recharacterised as an exemption from the requirement to measure investments in joint ventures in accordance with the equity method.

IFRS 11 Joint Arrangements

(b) IFRS 11 replaces the term 'shared decisions' introduced by ED 9 with the term 'joint control'. As in IAS 31, 'joint control' is one of the features that, along with the existence of a contractual arrangement, defines 'joint arrangements'.

(c) IFRS 11 classifies joint arrangements into two types—'joint operations' and 'joint ventures'. Each type of joint arrangement is aligned with a specific accounting requirement. ED 9 had classified joint arrangements into three types—'joint operations', 'joint assets' and 'joint ventures'.

(d) IFRS 11 provides application requirements to assist entities in the classification of their joint arrangements. The IFRS requires an entity to determine the type of joint arrangement in which it is involved by considering its rights and obligations. In particular, the IFRS requires an entity to give consideration to the structure and legal form of the arrangement, to the terms agreed by the parties in the contractual arrangement and, when relevant, it should also consider other facts and circumstances.

(e) IFRS 11 clarifies that not all the parties to a joint arrangement need to have joint control for the arrangement to be a joint arrangement. As a result, some of the parties to a joint arrangement might participate in the joint arrangement, but might not have joint control of it.

(f) The consensus of SIC-13 has been incorporated into IAS 28 (as amended in 2011), and SIC-13 is accordingly withdrawn. ED 9 had proposed to incorporate the consensus of SIC-13 into the standard on joint arrangements.

(g) The disclosure requirements have been placed in IFRS 12. ED 9 had proposed to incorporate the disclosure requirements for joint arrangements into the standard on joint arrangements.

(h) IFRS 11 does not require an entity to adjust the differences between the proportionate consolidation method and the equity method retrospectively when an entity changes from proportionate consolidation to the equity method when accounting for its joint ventures. Instead, it requires an entity to recognise its investment in a joint venture as at the beginning of the earliest period presented, by measuring it as the aggregate of the carrying amounts of the assets and liabilities that the entity had previously proportionately consolidated, including any goodwill arising from acquisition. ED 9 had proposed retrospective application of the requirements.

Cost-benefit considerations

BC71 The objective of general purpose financial reporting is to provide financial information about the reporting entity that is useful to existing and potential investors, lenders and other creditors in making decisions about providing resources to the entity. To attain this objective, the Board seeks to ensure that an IFRS will meet a significant need and that the overall benefits of the resulting information justify the costs of providing it. Although the costs to implement a new IFRS might not be borne evenly, users of financial statements benefit from improvements in financial reporting, thereby facilitating the functioning of markets for capital and credit and the efficient allocation of resources in the economy.

BC72 The evaluation of costs and benefits is necessarily subjective. In making its judgement, the Board considered the following:

(a) the costs incurred by preparers of financial statements;

(b) the costs incurred by users of financial statements when information is not available;

(c) the comparative advantage that preparers have in developing information, compared with the costs that users would incur to develop surrogate information;

(d) the benefit of better economic decision-making as result of improved financial reporting; and

(e) the costs of transition for users, preparers and others.

BC73 The Board concluded that the IFRS benefits preparers and users of financial statements. This is because the accounting for joint arrangements in the IFRS follows a principle-based approach. This approach has allowed the Board to remove the accounting option in IAS 31 so that each type of joint arrangement (ie 'joint operations' and 'joint ventures') is accounted for on a consistent basis. This contributes to enhancing the verifiability, comparability and understandability of these arrangements in entities' financial statements.

BC74 In the IFRS, the accounting for joint arrangements depends on the rights and obligations arising from the arrangement (not exclusively on whether the parties have chosen a particular structure or legal form to carry out their arrangements, or on the consistent application of an accounting policy—proportionate consolidation or equity method). Thus, the IFRS promotes greater comparability by applying the same approach to

IFRS 11 JOINT ARRANGEMENTS

different joint arrangements.

BC75   The Board believes that basing the accounting on the principles in the IFRS results in enhanced verifiability, comparability and understandability, to the benefit of both preparers and users. First, verifiability and understandability are enhanced because the accounting reflects more faithfully the economic phenomena that it purports to represent (ie an entity's rights and obligations arising from its arrangements), which allows them to be better understood. Second, requiring the same accounting for each type of arrangement will enable entities to account for joint arrangements consistently: arrangements that confer on the parties rights to the assets and obligations for the liabilities are joint operations and arrangements that confer on the parties rights to the net assets are joint ventures. Consistency in the accounting for joint arrangements will help to achieve comparability among financial statements, which will enable users to identify and understand similarities in, and differences between, different arrangements.

BC76   The Board noted that the costs that preparers will have to bear when applying the IFRS to their arrangements are concentrated in the assessment of the type of joint arrangement rather than in the accounting for the arrangements. This is because entities accounting for joint arrangements in accordance with IAS 31 were not required to classify their arrangements on the basis of their rights and obligations arising from the arrangement, but instead on whether the arrangement was structured in an entity. The IFRS will require entities to assess the type of joint arrangement in which they are involved when those arrangements have been structured through a separate vehicle. Even though the classification of the joint arrangements represents an additional assessment that was not required in IAS 31, the application requirements in the IFRS that should assist preparers in the classification of their arrangements are not unduly complex. The Board does not think that the additional assessment that the IFRS will require for the classification of arrangements will result in an undue cost to preparers.

BC77   The Board noted that the IFRS, by comparison with the exposure draft, simplifies the proposals by aligning the types of joint arrangement with the accounting methods. The Board concluded that once an entity has determined the classification of the arrangement, the accounting for the arrangement will follow accounting procedures that have not been modified by the IFRS (ie entities will either account for assets and liabilities or they will account for an investment using the equity method). However, the Board acknowledged that the requirement for joint operations to be accounted for in the same way in the entity's consolidated financial statements as in the entity's separate financial statements might lead to additional costs to entities in jurisdictions in which separate financial statements are required to be reported in accordance with IFRSs. This is because those requirements might cause entities to perform additional manual procedures such as reconciliations between the statutory accounts and the tax returns, and might require an entity to provide additional explanations of the impact of the changes to, for example, its creditors. Except for these costs and any other costs required on transition, the costs of accounting for joint arrangements once the entities have determined their classification will remain unchanged as a result of the IFRS.

BC78   The Board concluded that enhanced verifiability, comparability and understandability result in a more faithful representation of joint arrangements in the financial statements of the entities that are involved in such arrangements, and that those benefits outweigh the costs that preparers might incur when implementing the IFRS.

IFRS 11 Joint Arrangements
Illustrative Examples

IFRS 11 Joint Arrangements

Contents

1 CONSTRUCTION SERVICES	IE2 – IE8
2 SHOPPING CENTRE OPERATED JOINTLY	IE9 – IE13
3 JOINT MANUFACTURING AND DISTRIBUTION OF A PRODUCT	IE14 – IE28
4 BANK OPERATED JOINTLY	IE29 – IE33
5 OIL AND GAS EXPLORATION, DEVELOPMENT AND PRODUCTION ACTIVITIES	IE34 – IE43
6 LIQUEFIED NATURAL GAS ARRANGEMENT	IE44 – IE52

IFRS 11 JOINT ARRANGEMENTS

These examples accompany, but are not part of, IFRS 11. They illustrate aspects of IFRS 11 but are not intended to provide interpretative guidance.

IE1 These examples portray hypothetical situations illustrating the judgements that might be used when applying IFRS 11 in different situations. Although some aspects of the examples may be present in actual fact patterns, all relevant facts and circumstances of a particular fact pattern would need to be evaluated when applying IFRS 11.

Example 1 – Construction services

IE2 A and B (the parties) are two companies whose businesses are the provision of many types of public and private construction services. They set up a contractual arrangement to work together for the purpose of fulfilling a contract with a government for the design and construction of a road between two cities. The contractual arrangement determines the participation shares of A and B and establishes joint control of the arrangement, the subject matter of which is the delivery of the road.

IE3 The parties set up a separate vehicle (entity Z) through which to conduct the arrangement. Entity Z, on behalf of A and B, enters into the contract with the government. In addition, the assets and liabilities relating to the arrangement are held in entity Z. The main feature of entity Z's legal form is that the parties, not entity Z, have rights to the assets, and obligations for the liabilities, of the entity.

IE4 The contractual arrangement between A and B additionally establishes that:

(a) the rights to all the assets needed to undertake the activities of the arrangement are shared by the parties on the basis of their participation shares in the arrangement;

(b) the parties have several and joint responsibility for all operating and financial obligations relating to the activities of the arrangement on the basis of their participation shares in the arrangement; and

(c) the profit or loss resulting from the activities of the arrangement is shared by A and B on the basis of their participation shares in the arrangement.

IE5 For the purposes of co-ordinating and overseeing the activities, A and B appoint an operator, who will be an employee of one of the parties. After a specified time, the role of the operator will rotate to an employee of the other party. A and B agree that the activities will be executed by the operator's employees on a 'no gain or loss' basis.

IE6   In accordance with the terms specified in the contract with the government, entity Z invoices the construction services to the government on behalf of the parties.

Analysis

IE7   The joint arrangement is carried out through a separate vehicle whose legal form does not confer separation between the parties and the separate vehicle (ie the assets and liabilities held in entity Z are the parties' assets and liabilities). This is reinforced by the terms agreed by the parties in their contractual arrangement, which state that A and B have rights to the assets, and obligations for the liabilities, relating to the arrangement that is conducted through entity Z. The joint arrangement is a joint operation.

IE8   A and B each recognise in their financial statements their share of the assets (eg property, plant and equipment, accounts receivable) and their share of any liabilities resulting from the arrangement (eg accounts payable to third parties) on the basis of their agreed participation share. Each also recognises its share of the revenue and expenses resulting from the construction services provided to the government through entity Z.

Example 2 – Shopping centre operated jointly

IE9   Two real estate companies (the parties) set up a separate vehicle (entity X) for the purpose of acquiring and operating a shopping centre. The contractual arrangement between the parties establishes joint control of the activities that are conducted in entity X. The main feature of entity X's legal form is that the entity, not the parties, has rights to the assets, and obligations for the liabilities, relating to the arrangement. These activities include the rental of the retail units, managing the car park, maintaining the centre and its equipment, such as lifts, and building the reputation and customer base for the centre as a whole.

IE10 The terms of the contractual arrangement are such that:

(a)   entity X owns the shopping centre. The contractual arrangement does not specify that the parties have rights to the shopping centre.

(b)   the parties are not liable in respect of the debts, liabilities or obligations of entity X. If entity X is unable to pay any of its debts or other liabilities or to discharge its obligations to third parties, the liability of each party to any third party will be limited to the unpaid amount of that party's capital contribution.

(c)   the parties have the right to sell or pledge their interests in entity X.

(d) each party receives a share of the income from operating the shopping centre (which is the rental income net of the operating costs) in accordance with its interest in entity X.

Analysis

IE11 The joint arrangement is carried out through a separate vehicle whose legal form causes the separate vehicle to be considered in its own right (ie the assets and liabilities held in the separate vehicle are the assets and liabilities of the separate vehicle and not the assets and liabilities of the parties). In addition, the terms of the contractual arrangement do not specify that the parties have rights to the assets, or obligations for the liabilities, relating to the arrangement. Instead, the terms of the contractual arrangement establish that the parties have rights to the net assets of entity X.

IE12 On the basis of the description above, there are no other facts and circumstances that indicate that the parties have rights to substantially all the economic benefits of the assets relating to the arrangement, and that the parties have an obligation for the liabilities relating to the arrangement. The joint arrangement is a joint venture.

IE13 The parties recognise their rights to the net assets of entity X as investments and account for them using the equity method.

Example 3 – Joint manufacturing and distribution of a product

IE14 Companies A and B (the parties) have set up a strategic and operating agreement (the framework agreement) in which they have agreed the terms according to which they will conduct the manufacturing and distribution of a product (product P) in different markets.

IE15 The parties have agreed to conduct manufacturing and distribution activities by establishing joint arrangements, as described below:

(a) Manufacturing activity: the parties have agreed to undertake the manufacturing activity through a joint arrangement (the manufacturing arrangement). The manufacturing arrangement is structured in a separate vehicle (entity M) whose legal form causes it to be considered in its own right (ie the assets and liabilities held in entity M are the assets and liabilities of entity M and not the assets and liabilities of the parties). In accordance with the framework agreement, the parties have committed themselves to purchasing the whole production of product P manufactured by the manufacturing arrangement in accordance with their ownership interests in entity M. The parties subsequently sell product P to another arrangement, jointly controlled by the two parties themselves, that has been established exclusively for the distribution of product P as described below. Neither the framework agreement nor the contractual arrangement between A and B dealing with the manufacturing activity specifies that the parties have rights to the assets, and obligations for the liabilities, relating to the manufacturing activity.

(b) Distribution activity: the parties have agreed to undertake the distribution activity through a joint arrangement (the distribution arrangement). The parties have structured the distribution arrangement in a separate vehicle (entity D) whose legal form causes it to be considered in its own right (ie the assets and liabilities held in entity D are the assets and liabilities of entity D and not the assets and liabilities of the parties). In accordance with the framework agreement, the distribution arrangement orders its requirements for product P from the parties according to the needs of the different markets where the distribution arrangement sells the product. Neither the framework agreement nor the contractual arrangement between A and B dealing with the distribution activity specifies that the parties have rights to the assets, and obligations for the liabilities, relating to the distribution activity.

IE16 In addition, the framework agreement establishes:

(a) that the manufacturing arrangement will produce product P to meet the requirements for product P that the distribution arrangement places on the parties;

(b) the commercial terms relating to the sale of product P by the manufacturing arrangement to the parties. The manufacturing arrangement will sell product P to the parties at a price agreed by A and B that covers all production costs incurred. Subsequently, the parties sell the product to the distribution arrangement at a price agreed by A and B.

(c) that any cash shortages that the manufacturing arrangement may incur will be financed by the parties in accordance with their ownership interests in entity M.

Analysis

IE17 The framework agreement sets up the terms under which parties A and B conduct the manufacturing and distribution of product P. These activities are undertaken through joint arrangements whose purpose is either the manufacturing or the distribution of product P.

IE18　The parties carry out the manufacturing arrangement through entity M whose legal form confers separation between the parties and the entity. In addition, neither the framework agreement nor the contractual arrangement dealing with the manufacturing activity specifies that the parties have rights to the assets, and obligations for the liabilities, relating to the manufacturing activity. However, when considering the following facts and circumstances the parties have concluded that the manufacturing arrangement is a joint operation:

  (a) The parties have committed themselves to purchasing the whole production of product P manufactured by the manufacturing arrangement. Consequently, A and B have rights to substantially all the economic benefits of the assets of the manufacturing arrangement.

  (b) The manufacturing arrangement manufactures product P to meet the quantity and quality needs of the parties so that they can fulfil the demand for product P of the distribution arrangement. The exclusive dependence of the manufacturing arrangement upon the parties for the generation of cash flows and the parties' commitments to provide funds when the manufacturing arrangement incurs any cash shortages indicate that the parties have an obligation for the liabilities of the manufacturing arrangement, because those liabilities will be settled through the parties' purchases of product P or by the parties' direct provision of funds.

IE19　The parties carry out the distribution activities through entity D, whose legal form confers separation between the parties and the entity. In addition, neither the framework agreement nor the contractual arrangement dealing with the distribution activity specifies that the parties have rights to the assets, and obligations for the liabilities, relating to the distribution activity.

IE20　There are no other facts and circumstances that indicate that the parties have rights to substantially all the economic benefits of the assets relating to the distribution arrangement or that the parties have an obligation for the liabilities relating to that arrangement. The distribution arrangement is a joint venture.

IE21　A and B each recognise in their financial statements their share of the assets (eg property, plant and equipment, cash) and their share of any liabilities resulting from the manufacturing arrangement (eg accounts payable to third parties) on the basis of their ownership interest in entity M. Each party also recognises its share of the expenses resulting from the manufacture of product P incurred by the manufacturing arrangement and its share of the revenues relating to the sales of product P to the distribution arrangement.

IE22   The parties recognise their rights to the net assets of the distribution arrangement as investments and account for them using the equity method.

Variation

IE23   Assume that the parties agree that the manufacturing arrangement described above is responsible not only for manufacturing product P, but also for its distribution to third-party customers.

IE24   The parties also agree to set up a distribution arrangement like the one described above to distribute product P exclusively to assist in widening the distribution of product P in additional specific markets.

IE25   The manufacturing arrangement also sells product P directly to the distribution arrangement. No fixed proportion of the production of the manufacturing arrangement is committed to be purchased by, or to be reserved to, the distribution arrangement.

Analysis

IE26   The variation has affected neither the legal form of the separate vehicle in which the manufacturing activity is conducted nor the contractual terms relating to the parties' rights to the assets, and obligations for the liabilities, relating to the manufacturing activity. However, it causes the manufacturing arrangement to be a self-financed arrangement because it is able to undertake trade on its own behalf, distributing product P to third-party customers and, consequently, assuming demand, inventory and credit risks. Even though the manufacturing arrangement might also sell product P to the distribution arrangement, in this scenario the manufacturing arrangement is not dependent on the parties to be able to carry out its activities on a continuous basis. In this case, the manufacturing arrangement is a joint venture.

IE27   The variation has no effect on the classification of the distribution arrangement as a joint venture.

IE28   The parties recognise their rights to the net assets of the manufacturing arrangement and their rights to the net assets of the distribution arrangement as investments and account for them using the equity method.

Example 4 – Bank operated jointly

IE29   Banks A and B (the parties) agreed to combine their corporate, investment banking, asset management and services activities by establishing a separate vehicle (bank C). Both parties expect the arrangement to benefit them in different ways. Bank A believes that the arrangement could enable it to achieve its strategic plans to increase its size, offering an opportunity to exploit its full potential for organic growth through an enlarged offering of products and services. Bank B expects the arrangement to reinforce its offering in financial savings and market products.

IE30　The main feature of bank C's legal form is that it causes the separate vehicle to be considered in its own right (ie the assets and liabilities held in the separate vehicle are the assets and liabilities of the separate vehicle and not the assets and liabilities of the parties). Banks A and B each have a 40 per cent ownership interest in bank C, with the remaining 20 per cent being listed and widely held. The shareholders' agreement between bank A and bank B establishes joint control of the activities of bank C.

IE31　In addition, bank A and bank B entered into an irrevocable agreement under which, even in the event of a dispute, both banks agree to provide the necessary funds in equal amount and, if required, jointly and severally, to ensure that bank C complies with the applicable legislation and banking regulations, and honours any commitments made to the banking authorities. This commitment represents the assumption by each party of 50 per cent of any funds needed to ensure that bank C complies with legislation and banking regulations.

Analysis

IE32　The joint arrangement is carried out through a separate vehicle whose legal form confers separation between the parties and the separate vehicle. The terms of the contractual arrangement do not specify that the parties have rights to the assets, or obligations for the liabilities, of bank C, but it establishes that the parties have rights to the net assets of bank C. The commitment by the parties to provide support if bank C is not able to comply with the applicable legislation and banking regulations is not by itself a determinant that the parties have an obligation for the liabilities of bank C. There are no other facts and circumstances that indicate that the parties have rights to substantially all the economic benefits of the assets of bank C and that the parties have an obligation for the liabilities of bank C. The joint arrangement is a joint venture.

IE33　Both banks A and B recognise their rights to the net assets of bank C as investments and account for them using the equity method.

Example 5 – Oil and gas exploration, development and production activities

IE34　Companies A and B (the parties) set up a separate vehicle (entity H) and a Joint Operating Agreement (JOA) to undertake oil and gas exploration, development and production activities in country O. The main feature of entity H's legal form is that it causes the separate vehicle to be considered in its own right (ie the assets and liabilities held in the separate vehicle are the assets and liabilities of the separate vehicle and not the assets and liabilities of the parties).

IE35 Country O has granted entity H permits for the oil and gas exploration, development and production activities to be undertaken in a specific assigned block of land (fields).

IE36 The shareholders' agreement and JOA agreed by the parties establish their rights and obligations relating to those activities. The main terms of those agreements are summarised below.

Shareholders' agreement

IE37 The board of entity H consists of a director from each party. Each party has a 50 per cent shareholding in entity H. The unanimous consent of the directors is required for any resolution to be passed.

Joint Operating Agreement (JOA)

IE38 The JOA establishes an Operating Committee. This Committee consists of one representative from each party. Each party has a 50 per cent participating interest in the Operating Committee.

IE39 The Operating Committee approves the budgets and work programmes relating to the activities, which also require the unanimous consent of the representatives of each party. One of the parties is appointed as operator and is responsible for managing and conducting the approved work programmes.

IE40 The JOA specifies that the rights and obligations arising from the exploration, development and production activities shall be shared among the parties in proportion to each party's shareholding in entity H. In particular, the JOA establishes that the parties share:

(a) the rights and the obligations arising from the exploration and development permits granted to entity H (eg the permits, rehabilitation liabilities, any royalties and taxes payable);

(b) the production obtained; and

(c) all costs associated with all work programmes.

IE41 The costs incurred in relation to all the work programmes are covered by cash calls on the parties. If either party fails to satisfy its monetary obligations, the other is required to contribute to entity H the amount in default. The amount in default is regarded as a debt owed by the defaulting party to the other party.

Analysis

IE42   The parties carry out the joint arrangement through a separate vehicle whose legal form confers separation between the parties and the separate vehicle. The parties have been able to reverse the initial assessment of their rights and obligations arising from the legal form of the separate vehicle in which the arrangement is conducted. They have done this by agreeing terms in the JOA that entitle them to rights to the assets (eg exploration and development permits, production, and any other assets arising from the activities) and obligations for the liabilities (eg all costs and obligations arising from the work programmes) that are held in entity H. The joint arrangement is a joint operation.

IE43   Both company A and company B recognise in their financial statements their own share of the assets and of any liabilities resulting from the arrangement on the basis of their agreed participating interest. On that basis, each party also recognises its share of the revenue (from the sale of their share of the production) and its share of the expenses.

Example 6 — Liquefied natural gas arrangement

IE44   Company A owns an undeveloped gas field that contains substantial gas resources. Company A determines that the gas field will be economically viable only if the gas is sold to customers in overseas markets. To do so, a liquefied natural gas (LNG) facility must be built to liquefy the gas so that it can be transported by ship to the overseas markets.

IE45   Company A enters into a joint arrangement with company B in order to develop and operate the gas field and the LNG facility. Under that arrangement, companies A and B (the parties) agree to contribute the gas field and cash, respectively, to a new separate vehicle, entity C. In exchange for those contributions, the parties each take a 50 per cent ownership interest in entity C. The main feature of entity C's legal form is that it causes the separate vehicle to be considered in its own right (ie the assets and liabilities held in the separate vehicle are the assets and liabilities of the separate vehicle and not the assets and liabilities of the parties).

IE46   The contractual arrangement between the parties specifies that:

(a) companies A and B must each appoint two members to the board of entity C. The board of directors must unanimously agree the strategy and investments made by entity C.

(b) day-to-day management of the gas field and LNG facility, including development and construction activities, will be undertaken by the staff of company B in accordance with the directions jointly agreed by the parties. Entity C will reimburse B for the costs it incurs in managing the gas field and LNG facility.

(c) entity C is liable for taxes and royalties on the production and sale of LNG as well as for other liabilities incurred in the ordinary course of business, such as accounts payable, site restoration and decommissioning liabilities.

(d) companies A and B have equal shares in the profit from the activities carried out in the arrangement and, as such, are entitled to equal shares of any dividends distributed by entity C.

IE47 The contractual arrangement does not specify that either party has rights to the assets, or obligations for the liabilities, of entity C.

IE48 The board of entity C decides to enter into a financing arrangement with a syndicate of lenders to help fund the development of the gas field and construction of the LNG facility. The estimated total cost of the development and construction is CU1,000 million. ①

IE49 The lending syndicate provides entity C with a CU700 million loan. The arrangement specifies that the syndicate has recourse to companies A and B only if entity C defaults on the loan arrangement during the development of the field and construction of the LNG facility. The lending syndicate agrees that it will not have recourse to companies A and B once the LNG facility is in production because it has assessed that the cash inflows that entity C should generate from LNG sales will be sufficient to meet the loan repayments. Although at this time the lenders have no recourse to companies A and B, the syndicate maintains protection against default by entity C by taking a lien on the LNG facility.

Analysis

IE50 The joint arrangement is carried out through a separate vehicle whose legal form confers separation between the parties and the separate vehicle. The terms of the contractual arrangement do not specify that the parties have rights to the assets, or obligations for the liabilities, of entity C, but they establish that the parties have rights to the net assets

---

① In this example monetary amounts are denominated in 'currency units (CU)'.

of entity C. The recourse nature of the financing arrangement during the development of the gas field and construction of the LNG facility (ie companies A and B providing separate guarantees during this phase) does not, by itself, impose on the parties an obligation for the liabilities of entity C (ie the loan is a liability of entity C). Companies A and B have separate liabilities, which are their guarantees to repay that loan if entity C defaults during the development and construction phase.

IE51 There are no other facts and circumstances that indicate that the parties have rights to substantially all the economic benefits of the assets of entity C and that the parties have an obligation for the liabilities of entity C. The joint arrangement is a joint venture.

IE52 The parties recognise their rights to the net assets of entity C as investments and account for them using the equity method.